THE SECRET TO
CONSCIOUS LIVING

Accessing the Energy You Crave

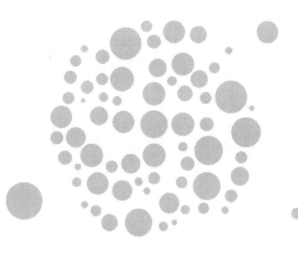

Matthew Joseph Anello

© 2015, Matthew J. Anello

ISBN-13: 978-0692351338 (A Well World Publications)

Library of Congress Control Number: 2014959358

A Well World Publications, Syosset, NY
1. SELF-HELP 2. Personal Growth 3. General

The Secret to Conscious Living: Accessing the Energy You Crave
Matthew J. Anello

Cover art by Kyle Shull
Layout by Sylvie Abecassis
Edited by Suzanne Boothby
Proofread by Matthew Lindberg-Work, d/b/a Solomon's Gap Productions
Printed by CreateSpace

DEDICATION

"This book is dedicated to the thousands of people who have allowed me in to their most private moments and darkest corners. These people have been, at various times, clients, friends, family and attendees at events I have been privileged to serve at."

TABLE OF CONTENTS

Introduction   **3**

Chapter 1   The Four Energy Magnifiers   **12**

Chapter 2   Don't Read This Book From Beginning to End   **27**

Chapter 3   Awareness Mode   **35**

Chapter 4   One Week Satisfaction Booster   **42**

Chapter 5   Let's Get Physical   **50**

Chapter 6   The Ocean of Emotion   **66**

Chapter 7   It's a Min(d)field   **81**

Chapter 8   The You Beyond Your Mind   **96**

Chapter 9   Committed Action Mode   **111**

Chapter 10   A Well-Oiled Machine   **124**

Chapter 11   Becoming Emotionally Fluent   **140**

Chapter 12   Mental Gymnastics   **154**

Chapter 13   Practicing Grace   **170**

Chapter 14   Epilogue   **179**

Resources & References   **182**

"Matthew is the real deal and a coach of the highest caliber. His commitment to your success is unwavering... like the steady flow of energy that will infuse your life as you embrace the secrets he shares with you in this guide."

— Marilena Minucci, MS, CHC, BCC, Creator, Quantum Coaching Method™

"Before I jumped into the book practice groups (while the manuscript was in progress) I was going through the motions of my coaching and speaking. After participating with this content, I had a clear gauge for where I was, where I wanted to be, and what I could do to get there. It helped me wake up. If you are in the personal growth fields, holistic healing or creative worlds, I highly recommend this book. I know the author walks his talk and the content rises from experiential and evolutionary personal practices."

— Seth Braun, Author of Indestructible Success

INTRODUCTION

Maybe you're on a crowded train checking emails. Maybe you're busily typing away on a report working from home. Maybe you're driving to meet up with friends, humming along to your favorite song of the moment. All is well. You're empowered, you're engaged and you're in the flow. Then, it happens. You get an email or text from a co-worker that pushes your buttons. Or, you start getting sleepy or become aware of tightness in your lower back. Perhaps you overhear a conversation nearby that distracts and disturbs you. Perhaps, you suddenly have the thought, "This job (or intimate relationship or friendship or...) is so **not** fulfilling me!"

Living in New York City in my mid 20's provided ample opportunity for situations like the above. If nothing else, NYC is a potent laboratory for self-development. That is, if you want to stay somewhat sane in that exciting, exasperating, chaotic city!

But I'll never forget the evening in 2001 that, in all likelihood, awoke me to my capacity to live a consciously created, satisfied and empowered life. It was the evening that I not only understood, but experienced that I could choose exactly how I was being, even if I couldn't always control the circumstances.

I had just completed one of my very first Ashtanga yoga classes at the home of the former HR director for the company I was working for. It was an intense class with lots of long holds in warrior 2 and a shoulder stand that seemed to last forever. And, in the end, I was basking in this new sensation that I can only describe as a "post-yoga high."

Now, I had already made plans to meet up with some friends at a bar for what would be a typical evening of drinking and socializing. But something was different. I got to the bar and it was the usual scene on any given night on the Lower East Side of Manhattan: lots of loud conversation, the latest hipster music emanating from the speakers and a group of friends ready to have a good time. Except this time, as I arrived, something was different.

Someone asked me what I was going to have to drink and I found myself saying, "Nothing right now." And then, much to my own surprise, I continued to socialize the rest of the evening without having even a sip of alcohol. And I had a blast! It is the very first time I can remember choosing my state of being in a social situation, rather than simply going with what I had always done before.

There were two key lessons I learned that night. The first is that there are activities I can engage with and habits I can form that create the foundation for profound shifts in how I experience my life. And the second is that, with that foundation in place, in any given moment, it's possible to be completely conscious *both* of what's happening for and around me, **and** the experience that I desire. These are what I call "meta moments" when I can actually generate an instantaneous shift in how a situation, evening or relationship goes. While it may sound like magic or "woo woo" to you, it is indeed possible and I promise you'll have greater access to these meta moments if you actively engage with the material in this book.

So, here's the bad news. Every day, for every single one of us, we will very likely experience dips in our energy, dips in our aliveness, interruptions that knock us off our game. We'll lose our connection to our innate capacity to be joyfully, fully alive and content and to be present in the moment. We forget to be *satisfied right now*. This experience is non negotiable if we're alive. There will be distractions and dips. And, it's particularly intense now in our communication-drenched, sped up era...which is only getting faster and faster. Every time this happens, we have a choice. Are we going to stay conscious and engage with life, or are we going to go numb and be distracted?

Now, here's the good news. Actually there are two particular pieces of good news that I'll be sharing with you in this book. The first one is this: We can strengthen and fortify our basic, innate capacity to bounce back from these setbacks, these interruptions... these disempowering episodes. And, engaging with the material in this book will have you working with the fundamental resources that power this strength. In fact, there are four Energy Magnifiers (EMs) that create a solid foundation for your capacity to generate satisfaction no matter what your external circumstances happen to be. Whether you know it or not, the degree to which you are nurturing these EMs determines your capacity to be resourceful in the face of both life's opportunities and life's challenges. I'll say a lot more about these EMs in the next chapter.

Ready for the second piece of good news? Here it is: While it's getting easier and easier to lose our connection and go unconscious there are also more and more ways to re-connect and re-engage! There are no shortages of methodologies, exercises and ideas for re-connecting. At this point in human history we now have access to thousands and thousands of books, written with great clarity and passion. In addition, many hundreds of gurus and organizations are out there doing amazing work, sharing their wisdom and insight with hundreds of thousands of people who are focused on living their best possible life.

And, if you're reading this right now, I'm going to assert that, for you, the fact that all of this wisdom exists out there is something you are aware of and appreciate. However, you're looking for something more. You're looking for applied wisdom. You're looking for personalized and relevant skill sets that you can apply to YOUR life, YOUR situation and YOUR future.

Well, then, you're in the right place. This book is designed to support you in leveraging the vast abundance of know-how and skill sets that already exist out there. You'll be introduced to a framework that's already been utilized by hundreds of people during the research phase for this book. This framework enables you to apply the knowledge of the four Energy Magnifiers (EMs) of life satisfaction to create a customized, flexible, ever changing, constantly evolving schema for your very own satisfied life experience.

You are given two profound, fundamental opportunities to experience a deep satisfaction while you are alive:

To know the awesome power you possess to respond powerfully to the biggest challenges that life throws at you *and then* to actually use that power to experience life the way that you want.

To cultivate living with humility, and in so doing, inspire others who are alive at the same time (and, if you really go for it, those that live after you).

Reading and applying the principles in this book will have you actively engaged with both of these opportunities.

It seems important to share with you that during the writing of this book, I experienced a stroke. What?!? Yup, you read that correctly. Why is this relevant? Well, while this was not something I would have asked for or that I was expecting, two notable aspects of the experience are relevant to what I want to communicate through this book.

The first notable aspect was the incredible physical, emotional, mental and spiritual resilience that those around me can confirm I displayed during, and after, the stroke. I credit all the work I've done with the EMs so far. Equally, I credit the support of the people with whom I've cultivated honest, loving, deep relationships with for this resilience. The doctors were concerned for my recovery, and yet recovery has been total. Not only that, but the actual experience of the stroke and the time after did not include any fear or pain.

The second is the important reminder that our learning and growing does not stop until we are dead (and maybe not even then!). Many people, including myself, were surprised that I would experience a stroke, given how much attention I've paid to my health over the years. What I can see is that I was given the opportunity to connect with a profound humility, which was actually empowering... as in, "I don't yet have it all figured out and perhaps I never will, yet that's okay!" Part of the humility is also experiencing, in a very real and immediate way, how I will always need others to move forward, no matter how much satisfaction I generate in my own life. We'll return to this idea of drawing on personally generated energy vs. engaging with others for that energy at various points in the book, so that you can bring a fresh approach to how you interact with others, via some practical tools and exercises.

Metaphor time! Generating a satisfied life is not an individual race, but something more like a multi-team relay. I invite you to envision a version of a relay race where multiple batons are being handed back and forth amongst members of "your" team (your immediate forebears/mentors/teachers and those you, in turn, support/inspire) **and** other teams. And the goal is that we all make it to the finish line with expanded awareness, not that only one person achieves the "most" awareness. The batons represent words of inspiration or acts of service.

Obviously, the stroke was a big wake up call. I am, even as I write this, considering how I can up my level of awareness so that I can move forward in a new way. The medical professionals are baffled as to what happened and why it happened. And, while they're working on figuring that out, I am looking to all four of the Energy Magnifiers because I know that this always yields powerful insights and more energy to move me forward.

You've heard this before in different ways and I'm here to reinforce it: It's not about getting your life right and/or perfecting your life, it's about re-remembering the fundamentals again and again and then turning the biggest challenges into new opportunities for growth and evolution. My personal experience is that there are no shortcuts to experiencing true, lasting satisfaction in life. And so, even though I didn't choose a stroke, I'm working with it, using the principles in this book.

Another way to think about this book is as a self-discovery handbook, designed to support you in learning what makes you tick. You'll learn about the entire universe that is you and you'll shift (slowly at first and faster as you continue) more and more of your average day into a state of what I like to call "alert calm."

I'd like to invite you to the most interesting event of your life. It starts whenever you choose and continues as long as you like. In fact, it doesn't have to end until the moment you die. It's an event called "Your Consciously Evolving Life" and the party starts now if you want it to. All you need to enjoy this party fully is to know where to look for all the energy you could ever need to dance your way through life. Much like any party, there's plenty of fun and enjoyment to be had if you know where to look and are willing to engage with everything that's happening and the people that are there. And, what's in it for you? Well, only the experience of giving yourself fully to the magic and flow of life instead of fighting for survival every day. Sounds good, right? Well, it's your birthright and it's time you claimed it.

My personal journey toward becoming aware of, practicing with, and choosing to master these EMs has been a long and winding one. I spent my first 24 or so years blissfully unaware of all of the resources I had available to me and clueless as to the forces around me that were influencing my day-to-day, hour-to-hour, and minute-to-minute state of being. Then a chance Reiki session at a wellness fair changed the course of my life. I was quite literally the last person the Reiki Master agreed to see. In fact, she worked with me *while* she was working with another person. And yet, I'll never forget the experience I had that afternoon. I experienced what can only be described as a bolt of energy escape from somewhere on the right side of my neck. And just like that, my awareness of the world and my self was changed forever.

This experience kicked off a flurry of changes in my life. I began to practice Ashtanga yoga. I went vegetarian. I began receiving a powerful form of chiropractic (Network Spinal Analysis) and even had a couple of years of therapy. As I began to incorporate and embody more and more of these disciplines (and many others), I could start to see an outline of the EMs and how critically important engaging with them was for my own journey.

I learned that my body was more than just something I needed to make as desirable as possible. Instead, it was a finely tuned machine that responded to my yoga practice by gifting me with a centered calm and clarity of thought. I learned that my emotions were not to be feared but instead embraced and even communicated to others, when and where appropriate. And that dwelling in and expressing these emotions, rather than being a dangerous proposition, could actually free me. I learned that my mind had been a mine-field of disempowered or limited thinking and that I could create new patterns of thought that were capable of not just imagining, but generating new life experiences and trajectories. And, I even learned how to connect to the part of me that was neither my thinking nor my feeling nor my body. I found the part of me that is not limited by mind, emotion or physicality. And I came to appreciate the great satisfaction that is available when I heed the messages from this realm and take action based on those messages in my life.

During this period of my life, I was introduced to the Energy Magnifiers. Since then, I've been at work on deepening and strengthening my relationship to each of them.

This book is written for those interested in living a life beyond the ordinary and the predictable. It offers tools for you to use in living your life that will challenge what could have been reasonably expected given your place of birth, upbringing, education, or past circumstances. If you can sense there is more to life than what you are currently experiencing, that it could be different, more authentic or more alive, this book is for you.

There are really two types of people who will find this text especially useful:

○ Those who are curious about new ways of empowering themselves and are new to the path of self-discovery.
○ Those who want to accelerate their growth and capacity to impact the well being of their family, friends or clients.

While this book will explore the full range of human experience from caring for our bodies to exploring our emotions to taming our minds to connecting to our soul, it is also meticulously practical. It will include philosophical discussion and intriguing concepts, but ultimately, the value of this book will be fully realized when you actually put it into action in your life, as you are currently living it. I will be encouraging you, regularly, to put the book down and apply the concepts in your reality. What you are generating, by engaging with the material in this book, is your personalized version of a life consciously lived; a life that satisfies you on every level imaginable and inspires you to be in the world, sharing yourself and your gifts with the rest of humanity. In order for you to have this kind of life, you will need to generate enough energy to make the shifts you need to make so that all of the important areas of your life are functioning at a high level and you are able to generate satisfaction for yourself on a sustainable basis.

I will ask you to take a comprehensive look at your life in total to become aware of what areas of life and what EMs of satisfaction you've been neglecting. In this way, you can begin to bring efficient focus that will deliver energetic results that are many multiples of the amount of energy you have put in. In effect, you're going to go on a holistic "diet for living." You'll be editing some thoughts, behaviors, and structures out and adding some in. You'll be regularly measuring and assessing your progress as you go. And, you'll be supported by the community of like-minded souls. Simply head over to "www.consciousliving.ning.com" to register and join this community.

Much like the Buddha encouraged, I ask that you do not take anything I have written here to be the truth on its face. Instead, I invite you to test out the various methods and experience first hand, the concepts in action. That way you can identify what resonates with you and make it work for you in your daily life. By the end, you'll not only have a toolbox, you'll also know which tools to use and when to use them, so that you can consistently and regularly generate a conscious experience of life for yourself. This will empower you to envision, generate and experience new futures that weren't available to you before engaging with yourself in this way.

So, why don't we get to know these energy sources? Read on to learn about the four EMs and why they're so fundamental.

CHAPTER 1

THE 4 ENERGY MAGNIFIERS

I t was a day that changed so much for so many. It's one that is burned into our collective and individual consciousness. On September 11th, 2001 I woke in Brooklyn and my sister and I walked to the subway station to head into Manhattan. The night before we had been together with our other sister for a rare evening when the "tripod" was in full effect. My sisters and I live full lives, and so, the times when all three of us are together are both rare and special.

We had enjoyed the Michael Jackson tribute concert at Madison Square Garden the previous evening and were now speeding toward Penn Station in a crowded underground subway. We commented on the shiny new subway cars that had just recently been introduced, with the digital displays, and I happened to look up at one of the new digital clocks at 8:46 a.m. and was commenting to my sister that we were just passing under the World Trade Center.

We arrived at Penn Station and began to realize that something big was happening as we glanced at the images on the TV screens of the smoking World Trade Center while briskly walking through the bustling masses. We tried to call our mother from both of our mobile phones and couldn't connect to the network. I got my sister on her train to

Philadelphia (we later learned that it was one of the last trains allowed out of NYC that day). I then got myself on the subway to head down to my office (where there was a landline available to me).

Not much of the rest of that day or the days that followed made much sense at the time. With time, distance and perspective, I can see that it was a turning point for me at a critical time in my life. In the months that followed I began learning to take the reins of my adult life and was generating new levels of satisfaction for myself. I tapped into a heightened desire to search out and master ways to generate more of the experiences that I wanted in this lifetime. I began expanding the forms of yoga I was practicing and made the choice to move into Manhattan from Brooklyn.

Perhaps the urgency of that day provided the necessary fuel for me to step boldly onto my true path, which has led all the way to the writing of this book. And perhaps the external chaos encouraged me to find a way to generate the inner energy required to meet the challenges of the world and each moment with presence and strength. My quest for the Energy Magnifiers that are available to all of us may just have begun on that fateful day.

It sounds so simple doesn't it? We hear it all the time from places as diverse as ancient texts to modern gurus to slogans on cheap t-shirts. "Be Present," "Be in the Now," "Enjoy the Moment." Oh yes, we think to ourselves...I must be more present in my life. Then I'll be able to enjoy myself more in each moment and I'll be enlightened, happy and satisfied. And it is simple. But let's not confuse simple with easy. ☺ As we distinguished earlier, there are so very many ways to distract ourselves these days. So, while getting present is still relatively easy, *staying* present is a lot more challenging.

Which begs the question: "What does it take to stay present?". The answer is two-fold. One, it takes practice. It's easy for children. They've not yet developed their full mental capacity and so there's a lot less "noise" in their space. You've seen them. They can get lost in a made-up game for hours. But for us adults, with 10, 20, 50 years of accumulated concepts, behavior patterns and practiced ways of being, we need to unlearn a LOT to get and stay present for more than 30 seconds.

Now, I'm going to say something here that I may not have been able to say had I published through one of the big publishing houses. I'm going to say it at the risk of possibly losing you as a reader after the next sentence. Here goes: Reading this book is not likely to significantly improve your day-to-day experience of living. While it's very likely that you'll have insights that will create shifts in the way you view things, without doing something different than you have been doing or shifting the way your life is organized, it's almost impossible to sustain a real, significant shift in your level of life satisfaction and consciousness. Perhaps you've come across that quote about the futility (some say insanity) of doing the same thing over and over yet expecting a different result? It's attributed to everyone from Einstein to the Narcotics Anonymous source text. One of the reasons this quote is repeated so often is because, for whatever reason, we all recognize that its part of human nature to resist making changes in our lives. Later in the book, there will be a chapter on the art and science of reliably implementing what you are becoming aware of in your day-to-day interaction with the EMs.

Okay, so now that you understand it's going to take some practice, what's the other needed element? Well, simply put, we need energy. While there is certainly abundant energy available in the universe, each one of us, if we don't pay attention, can deplete our individual storehouse of energy. This is because it's so very easy to give our energy away in little bits and pieces all day long. Our constantly thinking minds alone are such expert energy hogs. And then, the world around us is so seductively interruptive with a myriad of energy drains of every variety—from stressful external circumstances to our sometimes complicated and varied relationships with other people to disempowering patterns of mind chatter.

Every time we experience a circumstance as an obstacle or barrier instead of an opportunity, our energy is drained. For example, you can see a demanding boss as either an evil tyrant who is trying to squeeze ever last drop of productivity out of you OR you can see them as the perfect opportunity for you to examine where exactly you are going with your career.

In the realm of intimate relationship, you can see a challenge with your partner as a sign that something is wrong with him/her OR you can seize the opportunity to reveal more of yourself, go deeper into the depths of your psyche and create a whole new future with them based on this new understanding.

You can relate to a health challenge with disappointment at having gotten yourself in such a state OR you can be thankful that what hasn't killed you, will make you stronger and embark on a new course of action that will have you feeling better than ever in your body, even as you get older.

So you see, literally every dip in energy is an opportunity to learn something new and tap into new energetic resources.

Now, here's where you want to pay close attention. Whether or not you are aware of it, there are four fundamental *energy magnifiers* available to you at all times. These fountains of energy are available to each and every one of us and are with us at all times and wherever we are. I call them the Energy Magnifiers (or EMs). And we can be relating to these EMs of conscious living in any one of four different modes at different times.

While these energy magnifiers are available to all of us at all times, they do require a certain amount of our attention and energy in order for us to move from merely surviving to truly thriving. Luckily for us, when we put the appropriate amount of energy/attention in to them, they can become sustainable sources of energy and resilience. Even better, eventually, they have the capacity to transmute into magnifying glasses so that the energy output is greater than the energy you put in at any given moment. When an EM is in this energized state, our job is simply to bring our attention to it and "harvest" the energy that is emanating from it.

So, let's introduce each of these EMs. Throughout the rest of the book we'll be returning to them regularly to deepen, not just your understanding but your actual experience of leveraging them for the energy they contain.

BODY

We only get one and it needs to last us an entire lifetime, so let's start with the EM of our body. You can engage with this EM in three direct and powerful ways. First, via what nutrients we put into it (which literally creates each and every one of our cells, tissues and organs). Second, by focusing on increasing either strength or flexibility. And third, and probably most often forgotten, by caring for it. Let's look a bit deeper.

When we feed ourselves in a way that works for our unique needs, unnecessary strain is relieved (partly because all the systems that are tasked with removing unnecessary materials from the body can work on their natural cycle, rather than going into overtime). By paying attention to the unique food needs of our bodies, we are also fortifying and strengthening each and every cell, tissue, organ and system by providing the abundance of nutrients that they need (and less of what they don't) to run at an elevated and efficient level of functioning.

When we spend time maintaining or building strength and flexibility, our bodies supply us with everything we need to get us where we want to be on the planet with grace and an abundance of energy. And when we manage to find the right balance for us, right now, given the demands we place on our body at this point in our life, we are able to respond to the physical challenges of our day with gusto and ease.

And finally, there is the entire realm of actively and directly caring for our body. We're talking activities like massage, sauna, skin brushing and taking a nap. While many in our hyper-stimulated world consider these indulgences or luxuries (and some people reject that outright as something for "rich people" or "sissies"), we neglect them at the expense of having a relationship with our bodies that is intimate, profound and deeply nourishing. Not to mention, these activities feel really good. ☺

The great news is that if you are taking care of your body in all of these ways, building a strong foundation, you are then able to "tap in" to this EM at different times during your day and week for boosts of energy. Later on in the book, we'll take a much deeper dive into some of the ways you can leverage all of this available energy.

EMOTIONS

To be truly alive is to feel the full range of emotion available to us as human beings—from agony to ecstasy and everything in between. As many of us know, over the long term, suppressing our emotional expression is a recipe for dysfunction in relationships with others as well as a stressor for the body/mind.

So, how do we nourish this EM of conscious living? Well, first, we can practice becoming aware of our emotional state more and more of the time. Part and parcel with this awareness comes the experience of a widening range of emotion over the course of a given day or week. To be able to be truly present with the gift that is being alive, and then, minutes or hours later, being able to identify and feel a profound suffering (our own or someone else's) gives us access to the truth. And the truth is that we have the capacity to feel a broad range of emotion exactly *because* reality confronts us with a massive range of occurrences, people and situations. We need to be able to respond appropriately to all of them and with the right energy. It serves us to be capable of experiencing, fully and in the moment, whatever emotion is flowing through us. When we have this capacity, we can fully be with what's happening and take appropriate action.

Each time a shift is needed in our life, emotions come to both wake us up to this fact AND provide some of the energy and clarity to embrace that change.

One of my most prized mentors, Donald Epstein, speaks powerfully about emotions. He talks about how emotions are the body-mind's most effective way to move energy from one place to another. In fact, he talks about (e)motions as (e)nergy in motion. They have emerged as an evolutionary strategy so that we can respond to our life circumstances in a way that best assists us in responding to our environment and serves our future growth and evolution.

Let's take a dramatic example. Imagine someone in an emotionally abusive relationship. Their partner is constantly belittling them and berating them. In their mind they can think of many reasons to leave the relationship. But, they are not sure they have the energy to make the break and "go it alone." Enter the emotions. If this person were to connect to the full range and depth of their emotions, they would be more likely to have the capacity to express them, both with themselves and with those that care for them. They might then have the leverage to have what I referred to earlier in the book as a "meta moment" and courageously choose a new direction for their life.

In day-to-day life, it's much the same, on perhaps a smaller, less dramatic scale. Each time a shift is needed in our life, emotions come to both wake us up to this fact AND provide some of the energy and clarity to embrace that change.

Before we delve into the EM of the mind, let's look a bit at the interface of emotions and thoughts. It's important to distinguish your emotions from the thoughts that are almost invariably and seemingly inextricably linked to them. If you pay attention, you'll begin to notice that every time you feel an emotion, and especially when you feel a strong one, there is almost always an accompanying thought or series of thoughts that are associated with it. When you see this, you have an opportunity to do two things. One is to focus on only the emotion and actually feel it, rather than think about feeling it. And two, is that you can understand how you've collapsed these two distinct things (the emotion and the thought), and begin to look for other thoughts that you could connect to the very same emotion. This link is especially useful if you have combined emotion and thought in such a way that you have created a negative feedback loop of thought/emotion that is keeping you stuck.

Suppose you're on a conference call or in a meeting with 10 or so co-workers or colleagues. One particular colleague of yours says, "I'm not sure we have all the information we need here to make the best decision right now." You've been the one responsible for gathering the information necessary to have the meeting and so your immediate reaction is one of anger. And as soon as you feel that emotion, you have the thought, "That guy has it in for me and is trying to undermine me with our superiors." So, instead of feeling the emotion fully, and leveraging it for the energy it contains, you proceed to talk to two or three other colleagues about what went on in the meeting to get their perspective and then you go home and talk to your partner about it and over the next few days to 3 or 4 of your friends. In the end, you are left where you began, but actually slightly worse off. Now you're not only angry about what was said, you're also beginning to develop a reputation for being an office gossip or labeled as being "too sensitive."

Developing both a capacity to express our emotions with those around us and a skill set for communicating, responsibly, what is going on for us emotionally is profoundly honoring and nourishing.

So, what happened here? Well, to put it simply, you've collapsed an emotion with a thought. And by doing so, you've robbed yourself of both the energy available in the emotion and of the altered future that was possible. You see, if you experienced the emotion fully, you wouldn't feel quite such a strong tug to react to what someone has said. Instead, you'd feel the anger and then leverage that anger to actually *do something, say something or re-arrange something* so that what is not working for you (which triggered the anger) is less likely to happen moving forward.

When we begin to relate to emotions as signals and messages to create change rather than a signal to mindlessly react or, on the opposite end of the spectrum, get caught in an internal, disempowered dialogue, we generate new and far more effective outcomes in life.

And just one more thing: developing **both** a capacity to express our emotions with those around us **and** a skill set for communicating, responsibly, what is going on for us emotionally is profoundly honoring and nourishing. This is true both for ourselves and those around us. All these pieces of the emotional puzzle must come together 'just so' in order for us to have a true experience of living in a fully empowered and expressed way.

THOUGHTS

I don't know if you've ever experimented with writing down all of the thoughts that are running through your mind for a few minutes. If you haven't, I recommend you put down this book and spend the next four or five minutes writing down whatever it is that pops into your head. Ready? Go. No, really. Put down the book and type or write 'em out.

...Back? What you very likely have just become acutely aware of is that your mind is a minefield of random, chaotic, sometimes confused, sometimes quite negative thoughts. If your mind is anything like mine, it likes to focus in on anything that it perceives as a problem, so that it can go about keeping itself in business solving it.

The challenge with a chaotic mind is not so much that it's chaotic, but that we are mostly unaware of the chaos. Our level of life satisfaction is impacted profoundly when this chaos is allowed to continue, unchecked, for hours, days and weeks. Does the chaos persist so that the mind can have something to do? And, here's the even more painful part. Oftentimes, our minds tell us *we* are the problem. As in, a thought that goes something like "you're not smart enough" or "you better be careful putting yourself out there" or "are you sure you can handle this?"

Don't believe me? I've got another quick writing exercise for you. Identify the area of your life that you are currently least satisfied with. It could be your career, your intimate relationship, your finances, your health. Really, anything. It just needs to be an area of life that you are not currently experiencing the level of satisfaction you know is possible.

Now, do that same exercise you just completed, again.

...How many of the thoughts were positive, empowering and uplifting? Now, don't misunderstand me. The intention in cultivating and fortifying the realm of mind is not to be engaged in so-called "positive thinking." Instead, the aim is to develop the capacity to identify when we are in disempowered states of being so that we can acknowledge it, see clearly what it was that landed us in that state of being, and then chart a course out with speed and certainty. This requires an increase in our level of awareness and a willingness to engage with aspects of our thinking that can be uncomfortable and challenging to be with. But the rewards are many.

HIGHER SELF

And, finally, there is the part of us that exists beyond our thoughts. Cultivating a relationship with this aspect of ourselves has often been an endeavor we have ceded to those affiliated with the world's religions. That said, whether or not you currently affiliate yourself with an organized religion, developing a strong connection to the part of you that exists beyond your thinking mind, beyond the coming and going of your emotions, and beyond the current condition of your physical body can be a profound source of energy, motivation and inspiration as you navigate through life...if you allow it.

And, for those, who, for whatever reason, are less comfortable with or less inclined to seek out this connection, there are ways in which you can engage with your soul/spirit in a way that is tangible, practical and embodied.

In order to give you a taste of what's available beyond the mind, there is a very simple exercise you can do. Simply close your eyes, and, for as long as you can, observe yourself breathing in and breathing out. For some people, it can be helpful to say to yourself during the exercise "inhale, exhale, inhale, exhale."

Now, here's the key piece. You will need to bring particular attention to the space between the inhales and exhales. In these moments, when nothing is happening, you have access to what's beyond your mind. And then, for some people, as they do this exercise, it's helpful to bring awareness to the fact that there is nothing you actually need to do in order to keep breathing. If you can completely relax into this reality, you might enjoy the profundity of the truth:

You are something much bigger and broader than is currently embodied.

A wordless sense of wonder begins to bloom in your mind.

Now that you have been introduced to these Energy Magnifiers (Body, Emotions, Thoughts, and Self), let's explore some of the ways that you can engage with them.

First, let's take a look at what it can look like to have a narrow focus on just one EM for the majority of the time. For example – You have very likely come across different people in your life who are laser focused on each of the individual EMs, almost to the exclusion of the others. In fact, in many ways, they may have mastered the art of squeezing that particular EM for all the energy it has to offer.

So, you may have someone in your life who is deeply committed to their physical health and well being. They are always up to date with the latest fitness routines, are well versed on all of the newest super food discoveries and are the first one to jump at the opportunity for a spa weekend with their friends. This person is milking the body EM for all it's worth and is constantly looking for another way to squeeze even more from it.

You may also know someone in your family, or perhaps a friend, who seems to always be experiencing some kind of emotional drama. They are either ecstatically high or deep down in the dumps, but no matter what the day, they are feeling something intensely and wanting to share about it with the people around them. It seems that their day is not complete unless they've felt at least five different emotions, three of them super intensely, and have told at least 10 people about the experience.

Or, maybe you know someone who meticulously plans her day, week and month out in advance. They prepare themselves rigorously for each and every important interaction they will have with someone by thinking through exactly what they want to say and imagining all the possible responses so they can be prepared for those too. They are constantly absorbing all the latest research, information and articles about any topic they are interested in and are happy to talk with you for hours about it.

And then, you might know someone else in your life who doesn't let a day go by without meditation for more than an hour. They write in their gratitude journal religiously and spend the majority of their waking hours volunteering their time at various charities or caring for family members and catering to the needs of their friends.

Now here's the thing. We can't blame someone for engaging with a EM in this way. They are simply doing what they know to do to generate sufficient energy to navigate their life. And, mastering one of the EMs can bring great benefits! The thing is that focusing on just one fosters rigidity and, ultimately, limits what's possible. Having the perfect body without cultivating the mind leaves one with a reduced range of options in life. While certain doors of opportunity will swing open widely, others will remain forever locked. The same is true for obsessing over any of the other EMs.

Here's another way to think about it. Think about all that it takes to keep a car running well. While you can get around for a long time simply filling up the gas tank when it gets near empty, you'll have a hard time seeing where you're going if you haven't topped up the windshield wiper fluid. And you'll be in for a rude surprise one day when your car doesn't start because you haven't changed the oil in more than 30,000 miles. This is akin to what it's like focusing on just one EM. You'll be able to survive, but you certainly won't be thriving. And much like a car running on old oil, you won't be operating at peak efficiency. If the windshield has not been cleaned in some time, your view of life and your world will tend to narrow and remain cloudy.

If we want to live our life "in the flow" and experience the true magic of living, we need to be able to effectively tap into multiple energized EMs in a given day. In order to be able to do this, we need to first be aware of the current energy state of each of the EMs and then know which EMs to focus on, how to most effectively engage them, and finally, when to "sequence" our attention or engage with two EMs at one time, so that we leverage an energized EM to help us boost one that's less than energized.

Now, I can almost hear you thinking, "Matthew, this sounds like a lot of work!" Well, while this may seem like an awful lot to be aware of and engaging with, I promise you it gets easier with time. And, initially, you'll only be consciously engaging with one (or at most two) EMs at any given time. In fact, by the time you are engaging all four EMs regularly, it won't be something that will feel at all like effort or work. Instead, you will be so satisfied with how you are living your life, and be so clear as to what the source of that satisfaction is, that you would laugh at the idea of going back to how you were before you started working with the EMs in your life.

So, let's recap what we've discussed so far. In order for us to be fully present more often in our lives we require two things: we need to practice getting present and we need a sufficient amount of energy to get and stay present. This book is designed to be the kick off for (or boost to your already existing) practice. And, the EMs are the already existing, limitless sources of energy. But, what's the ultimate goal here? Why be present? Because only in "being present" can you experience genuine life satisfaction. You see, being satisfied in life is not actually about what you have, who is near you or even whether you are happy or not. Being satisfied in life is the capacity to: 1) shift your state of being (or, said another way, how you are experiencing any given moment) and 2) remain empowered no matter how a particular situation, day, or week goes for you.

You see, when you have cultivated a sufficient degree of presence in your life, satisfaction is the majority of your experience and no external circumstance has power over you. Instead, you are able to "resource yourself" whenever necessary to evolve and transform into the next version of yourself, based on what you now want and based on the changes occurring in your environment (including, but not limited to: shifting relationships, changing economic climates and unexpected health challenges). You experience every challenge or "negative situation" as the next piece of fuel for growth and evolution.

When you are living this way, simple happiness is no longer the goal. What if chasing after the emotional state of happiness is exactly what's keeping you from experiencing happiness more often? What if the emotion of happiness isn't actually meant to be lasting? What if there is a human experience that's much deeper and more sustainable?

Well, it turns out there is. It's called being satisfied. You'll notice I'm not referring to satisfaction solely as an emotion. I'm describing it as a state of *being*. Satisfaction lasts longer than any given emotion you may be feeling because the state of *being satisfied* relies on more than just the emotion of being happy. It requires more because it offers more. More on that a bit later...

Now, I don't want you to confuse satisfaction with laziness. The idea is not to get to a place where you are no longer striving, growing, and evolving and instead are sitting on the couch with a full belly, surveying your domain and all the creature comforts you've collected. Quite the opposite. Satisfied living requires your active participation and focused attention and requires you to remain hungry. Hungry for building the kind of life that involves lots of risk and lots of reward. Why? Because being truly satisfied means having left nothing unexplored. Nothing unexamined. Nothing left undone. Just one more note on the body EM, and really, all of the EMs. For each of them, in what ways, how frequently and how intensely you are interacting with them will fluctuate based on where you are at in life. Remember, this party lasts your entire life. You'll want it to ebb and flow.

SO NOW, WHERE TO BEGIN?

THE FOUR MODES OF ENGAGEMENT

Before we go any further into how to actually engage with your EMs, it's important to understand the four different modes you can be in when it comes to engaging with them.

The first mode is the one you're in if you're simply not consciously engaging with the EMs at all. We'll call this the *unconscious mode*. The thing is, even if you are in this mode, you are being influenced by the EMs. You just are not able to respond to the messages because you are not aware that you have the capacity to do so. These messages will register in your awareness as mysterious and seemingly random drops and surges of energy. Take note: as much as the EMs are always available to us as limitless sources of vitality and energy, we do best by being consciously connected with them. And while your subconscious may guide you, here and there, toward sufficient connection, there is simply too much else going on around us to ensure a steady, strong connection to all four EMs at the level required/desired.

Or, you can be in *awareness mode*, which is to say that you are actively learning about and being receptive to the signals that you are receiving (from either within or without). You are expanding and deepening your awareness of what the messages are, how they apply to you and how to begin to take action to move from a state of relative stagnation in dissatisfaction to one of increasing satisfaction.

At some point, you have received enough information and want to now engage with these energies in such a way that they fuel your own personal transformation or fuel a shift in the world around you that you feel compelled to generate. This is *committed action mode*. It's in this mode that people commit to a long term and significant shift in eating habits, exercise routine, relationship status, or spiritual practice.

And there is also another state that some of us aspire to and achieve. It's the path of mastery. It's the state in which you are now able to reap the rewards of time, effort and focus placed on listening for, decoding and taking action to fortify and strengthen your relationship with one or more of the EMs. When you are engaging with the EMs in this way, you are in mastery mode.

With this book, we will be focusing solely on the awareness and committed action modes. It is my intention that by focusing on these modes, those who might be in unconscious mode will be moved into one of these other two modes. And as for you masters out there, any master worth his weight in salt knows that the only way to truly be in mastery mode is to be willing to regularly re-visit the awareness and committed action modes. ☺

Just one more note about the EMs. They are a dynamic and interrelated system. They can fuel one another. They can drain one another. They can combine in many ways to enhance the depth of your experience of life. So, we´ll discuss these dynamics in a chapter that is devoted to walking you, step by step, through the process of shifting this material from conceptual to applied.

Finally, I want to mention that there are some longer term life cycles that we each move through that increase or decrease the "volume" (both in terms of degree of intensity and in terms of amount) of the messages being delivered from each EM. While interesting and illuminating in time, the purpose of this book is primarily to first get you acquainted with and leveraging the EMs. So, when you get to the epilogue, you'll see that I begin to address the details of this longer-term cyclicality. And, I know enough to know that I'm no expert on this longer-term cyclicality as a 39 year old.

CHAPTER 2

DON'T READ THIS BOOK FROM BEGINNING TO END

Have you struggled in the past to effect lasting change in your level of life satisfaction or wondered why certain behavior patterns have been so stubborn? Me too. I've developed a visual representation of what I have observed in my own life and the lives of the people that I've coached that I hope will help you to understand how this can happen and support you in more fully tapping into your true potential.

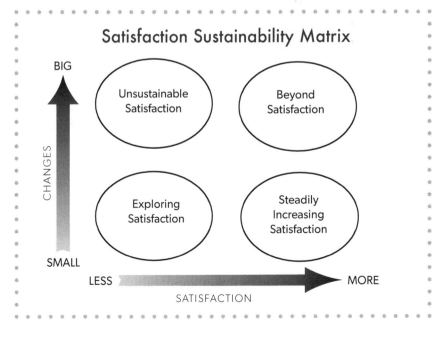

Satisfaction Sustainability Matrix

I developed this model in response to two of the most fascinating questions that emerged as I coached many hundreds of people toward greater degrees of life satisfaction. First, I got really interested in why some of the people I was coaching seemed to make progress more easily and swiftly than others. And second, why were some people able to make changes and increase their level of life satisfaction, but then were unable to sustain it? As I considered it, it became very clear that there were actually four different places you could be on any change-making journey in life. When I saw this, it illuminated much of the "why" behind these questions.

As you can see, this model illustrates the relationship between the size of the changes you are making (on the "up/down" axis) and the level of life satisfaction you are experiencing (on the "left/right" axis). You can think about the left/right axis as a scale from 1-10 in your current degree of satisfaction in a particular area of your life. And the up/down axis is a measure for the relative size or magnitude of change you are making in that area. For example, if you're focused on the world of health and you begin drinking a 12-oz glass of lemon water every morning upon waking (toward the bottom of the axis), that's a far cry from going cold turkey vegetarian, organic and local all at once (very close to the top of the axis).

Before we get into detail about the four different places you can be when you are focused on changing an area of your life that is not satisfying for you, you should know that there is actually a fifth place you can be. You see, this model is designed to provide clarity for people that are actively interested in generating a shift in their level of satisfaction in one or more areas of their life. For all of us, almost all of the time, there are certain areas of life where we are simply not actively engaged with or focused on impacting our satisfaction level. This fifth place is where we are when we're not actively engaged with increasing our level of satisfaction in an area of life. For example, you may be super focused on the realm of intimate relationship while also taking significant action around your health and finances but simply not be actively engaged in the realm of your career. Or sometimes, we're on auto-pilot in many areas of life and only really focused on shifting one. And some people are simply not interested in actively and consciously engaging with their level of life satisfaction. If you have gotten this far reading this book, I assure you that you are not one of those people. ☺

Let's begin exploring the different places you can be according to this model by taking a look at Unsustainable Satisfaction. We often experience this place multiple times before we make real progress in an area of life that we are dissatisfied with. I suspect you will likely recognize what it looks like in your life when you're in this place. It's that experience you have when you have tried to make a large change in an area of your life or with a certain behavior with very little preparation. Typically, your level of understanding about why you find yourself in your current set of circumstances and your level of clarity about what is the best way for you to sustainably move out of it are both quite low. The outcome is that success, much beyond an initial burst, is very unlikely.

A great example of a common experience of Unsustainable Satisfaction is nearly the entire experience that people have with dieting. Whether it's a New Year's Resolution to finally kick the daily chocolate habit or a sudden scramble to shape your body into something that you feel comfortable showing off at the beach, most people have not done the deeper and sustained work necessary to set themselves up for success when they attempt to make the shift. We'll be discussing what is really necessary, and how to go about it, in much further detail in Chapters 3 and 4.

... sometimes, we're on auto-pilot in many areas of life and only really focused on shifting one.

There is one caveat when considering this idea of large changes not being sustainable. I want to be clear that I am not suggesting that big changes don't occur or that they don't sometimes occur suddenly or unexpectedly. What I am suggesting is that the only way those big changes can sustain themselves is with a sufficiently developed relationship with the Energy Magnifiers and a history that includes a period of Exploring Satisfaction and a period of Steadily Increasing Satisfaction. Now let's take a look at these first two phases.

When you're Exploring Satisfaction, you are conscious that your level of satisfaction is not as high as you want it to be in a particular area of life and you are busy actively making small changes to address this. When you're in this phase you are a sponge for both new information and regularly applying that information to your life in small ways. You are trying things out to see both what makes sense for you in practice and what methods and models work to move you in the direction of greater satisfaction.

The pitfall in this mode is "jumping the gun" and bouncing up into Unsustainable Satisfaction by making a big change before you have a sufficient level of awareness. This is not necessarily a bad thing, it's just that it returns you back to Exploring Satisfaction and can be a time waster. It also has the unfortunate side effect of disempowering many people and taking the wind out of their sails when it comes to inspiration and excitement to reach their goals. Much more about this in Chapter 9.

The idea with this phase of Exploring Satisfaction is that you're actively exploring an area of life and how you relate to it. And, you're engaging with the small changes that, over time, accumulate and have a kind of multiplier effect. Ultimately, as you engage in Exploring Satisfaction, you are moving along the axis from less to more in the realm of satisfaction. So, the idea is to "graduate" from Exploring Satisfaction towards Steadily Increasing Satisfaction.

So, let's take a closer look at Steadily Increasing Satisfaction. You know you are operating in this phase in an area of life when you are experiencing a high degree of satisfaction. Maybe you're at a 7, 8, or 9 in your satisfaction assessment of an area of your life. Things are really humming along for you, you're satisfied and you're enjoying your experience.

You may wonder how it is that you got to this place. What's happened is that, either consciously or unconsciously, you have continuously been making tweaks and small changes to this area of your life to expand even further your level of satisfaction in that area.

I like to use an example from my own life in the area of health and well-being to illustrate the experience in this phase. When it comes to my health and well-being, I am highly satisfied. I have sufficient energy to power all of the activities and conversations that I want to get involved with in a given day, week or month. And my level of health, as measured by sick days and the core metrics of health that the medical world uses, is superb.

While that's all well and good, what's valuable to look at is: How did I create this? And the answer is that I've been actively at work on my health and well-being for almost 15 years now. When I look back on the past 15 years, I notice that I regularly made small changes and tweaks to continue to expand or even just maintain my health. Most of the time it was something as simple as changing what kind of milk I put on my cereal or making some minor modification to the number of times I practice strength training vs. yoga during a given week.

What I also noticed is that the long, steady focus was punctuated by bursts of much larger changes. There were times when I totally shifted the kind of yoga I was practicing or started eating meat again after being vegetarian for 3+ years. These bursts of much more significant change were actually great demonstrations of the final phase that's left for us to explore.

Beyond Satisfaction is, I believe, ultimately what we are all striving for. This phase is really only accessible if you follow the "Yellow Brick Road" all the way from Exploring through to Steadily Increasing and finally, Beyond. When we're operating in this phase, there's nothing to improve, nothing to fix and nothing to strive toward. Instead, we're really enjoying the fruits of all of our previous labors and choosing to open ourselves up to totally new experiences in a particular area of life.

Because we've already expanded our awareness and made a significant number of small changes that have compounded and multiplied in their effects, we are now able to take a large leap, and do so sustainably. It can take years to gain access to this phase, but when you do, every second of effort and focus is so very worth it.

As I was sharing with you before, health & well-being is an area of my life where I am highly satisfied. Most of the time, I am operating in the Steadily Increasing Satisfaction phase. But then, occasionally, I pop up into Beyond Satisfaction. One recent example in my life was my re-introduction to the world of swimming. I had spent many summer mornings in my youth learning all of the major strokes and had even gotten myself to a level where I could begin training as a lifeguard. But then, for whatever reason, life took me in a different direction and, while I still swam at the ocean or briefly in pools during the summer, I largely left my training in the past.

Then, in my late 30's, I moved to Barcelona, where the sun is plentiful. I made friends with people who were part of a swim team that offered training and opportunities to compete in different cities across Europe, So, I decided to give it another go! And while, of course, there's lots to learn (and re-learn) and plenty of barriers to break through, all of the other awareness and actions I've taken over the years around my health and well-being have set me up very powerfully to "dive in" to this new sport. And, more than that, I've been able to incorporate this new sport into my weekly routine while still maintaining focus on yoga and strength training, and making modifications to my diet to support the new level of activity.

What's particularly magical about having access to the experience of being Beyond Satisfaction is the capacity to engage in completely new ways in that area of life "just because." It's the experience of being able to do or experience something just for the pure joy or excitement, or really no reason at all, and gain something from that experience. I submit to you that this is the life you

The very act of engaging in awareness and committed action modes will help shift the degree of satisfaction from an unsatisfactory level to a satisfactory one.

want to be living and the one that is your birthright. It's actually how life was for you for the first few years on the planet, when everything was new, exciting and awe-inspiring. You can reclaim that experience again, now, and this book will give you the tools to do that.

It's my intention in sharing this model with you, that you have a sense for the big picture when it comes to cultivating and manifesting a life that is deeply satisfying. And beyond that, a life that becomes more and more of an adventure and less and less of a struggle to "improve" yourself or your circumstances. To that end, there is a way that the modes of engagement from the previous chapter relate to this model that is important to note.

As discussed in the last chapter, this book is designed to empower you in both awareness mode, where you see what needs attention in an area of life that's not working for you, and committed action mode where you devote yourself to shifting into a new state. *Both* of these modes reside in the phase of Exploring Satisfaction. The very act of engaging in awareness and committed action modes will help shift the degree of satisfaction from an unsatisfactory level to a satisfactory one. This shift then opens up your access to Steadily Increasing Satisfaction, when you continue to make tweaks and changes in an increasingly easy and natural way. Finally, you experience a deep enough connection to the Energy Magnifiers to be able to blast off into the phase of Beyond Satisfaction.

It's important to remember that you are very likely in different phases in different areas of your life at different times. And, it's very common to have more than one area of life that's currently bouncing back and forth between Exploring and Unsustainable Satisfaction modes. You can tackle one area of life at a time by engaging in Awareness Mode for as many weeks as is necessary in order to provide you with the insight and experience needed to move decidedly into Committed Action mode in that area of life. The next chapter is designed to provide you with the guidance and focus needed to do just that.

During the research phase for this book, many people who participated on the tele-seminars had multiple areas of life that were functioning in a less than satisfactory way. The question would often come up as to which area to tackle first. The good news is that increasing your level of awareness and/or committed action in *any* area of life is going to positively impact other areas of your life as well. And so, you are welcome to go with your gut instinct and begin with whichever area of life you can see is going to make the most overall difference to your level of overall life satisfaction. Even if you choose incorrectly, you can simply switch to another area and utilize the process outline in Chapter 4 to re-direct your attention to where you can derive the most benefit.

At this point, I trust you are beginning to get excited about the changes that are available to you when you apply the concepts and philosophies of this book. And, excitement is a good thing. Really, it's a great thing. But it is just not going to be enough to realize the shifts you want to see. In order for your reality to shift, significantly and sustainably, you will need to spend your time differently and you will need to be willing to try things that, under every day, "normal" circumstances, you would never do. To that end, each of the individual chapters on the EMs will include exercises for you to choose from. Some of these exercises may, at first, seem odd or even uncomfortable. I encourage you to try them anyway and be open to being surprised by what they can show you.

I really invite you to bring a sense of curiosity to the endeavor. I will offer you the very best of the tried and true methods I have used to empower many thousands of people around the world. The thing is, if you're not up for being curious and open minded about something and come from a place of already knowing what an exercise or process will provide or not provide, the book might be an interesting and thought provoking read. However, reading it alone will not likely deliver the tangible, day-to-day shift in your lived experience that you are truly looking for. The good news is, there is an online community that exists alongside this book to support you in creating the shifts you want to experience. Head over to consciousliving.ning.com to request to be added to the community.

CHAPTER 3

AWARENESS MODE

I f you think about it, any shift you have made in the way you live your life started with an initial awareness that something needed to change. It may have been a conversation you had with a friend or a realization you had on your own, after taking a momentary step back from your life as you're currently living it. Sometimes the awareness that a shift is desired is completely unexpected, and sometimes you've been aware of the need on some level but didn't feel it was important enough to give your full attention to.

No matter how you have become aware of this desire to change, when we have determined or realized that we are in awareness mode for a particular EM, the first thing to get is the *way of being* that will empower you to maximize your time in this mode. You want to get profoundly curious. Let your primary question be something along the lines of, "What is something new that I can learn here?" So, what we're going to be exploring in this chapter are some very simple and practical ways to increase our level of self-awareness. This will include mini exercises that give you just a taste of what's to come later in the book.

Once you've developed a sufficient level of awareness, the next thing to grasp is that small steps get you much farther in the long term than big leaps. Think the tortoise and the hare. You're looking for simple, effective ways to build your capacity to tune in to what's happening with a particular EM. So, as your awareness expands and deepens, what will begin to become obvious is that the messages from your body, emotions, mind and higher self are pointing you in a particular direction. Once you become aware of this, you can begin to move in that direction deliberately by engaging more vigorously with the EM's to generate sufficient energy to move forward.

You see each Energy Magnifier requires a certain baseline amount of energy (in the form of our attention, focus and deliberate action) in order to keep us functioning in our lives. This baseline amount of energy is the pre-requisite for (later on) being able to engage with the EMs in their highly energized state as sources for energy and conscious living.

What does awareness look like in day-to-day living? Let's take the example of our bodies. During any given day the body has an array of needs that we may or may not be conscious of. The most fundamental of these needs are oxygen and water. Have you ever noticed the difference it makes in your level of energy when you step outside after being in an enclosed space for too many hours? That rush of fresh air likely contains a higher percentage of oxygen and your body responds almost immediately. You may notice that the level of tension in your body decreases and that your thinking becomes clearer. This is a perfect example of how paying attention to one of the EMs can positively impact another.

The thing is, your body has a limited number of methods for getting your attention. Beyond pain, hunger and a dry mouth, the signals can be very subtle. Tightness in the shoulders can be building for hours before you notice it. So, it takes something to build up your level of awareness and to get the patterns of behavior in place that allow for regular check-ins with your body as to what its current needs are. A good time to start is right now! Put this book (or digital device) down and ask yourself the following questions:

Body Awareness Questions

- ❍ What is my body asking for right now?
- ❍ What would feel best to do for my body right now?
- ❍ Could my body benefit from a glass of water?
- ❍ Could my body benefit from a 1-minute mini stretching session?

Just setting a reminder to ask yourself these questions even 3 times per day can revolutionize your capacity to be present, energized and alert.

But why stop there with so many more EMs to tap into? :)

The next opportunity for increasing your level of self-awareness is by tuning into your emotional state. If you really consider it, how often during the day are you allowing yourself the space, even for 30 seconds, to simply feel what you are feeling? When we don't allow ourselves this space, pent up emotions can be energy vampires, slowly draining you without you even knowing it. As you may already be aware, emotions that you don't allow yourself to feel in the moment they arise get stored away in the body-mind. And it takes energy to keep them in there, waiting for you to fully feel them. The more frequently you can give your body-mind a chance to feel, the less energy it needs to waste storing them.

We waste energy at least two different ways when we're not allowing ourselves to feel our emotions. One is that the body can tighten and close down in places. The Somato Respiratory Integration (SRI™) work that I've done with people for the past 8 years has given me ample opportunity to observe the impacts of either a lack of awareness or a lack of willingness to acknowledge emotions we are feeling. I've seen, up close and personal, with both myself and the thousands of people I've worked with, how unexpressed emotion limits the range of motion in the body and the ability to even stay present with the body.

I'm not simply referring to our ability to stretch our muscles and the range of motion of our joints. I'm talking about the capacity to focus on a particular area of the body and bring full attention and focus there. What I have observed is that when we can be with all parts of our physical body, we have access to the full range of our emotions as well.

The second way that we can waste energy is by shunting emotional energy up into the mind. When this happens, instead of actually feeling the emotion that we're feeling, we get interested in why the emotion is happening and what it means. This action gets the mind going and once the mind gets going, it's challenging to interrupt it. Thus, we end up spending all manner of mental energy rather than simply experiencing the emotion, and in the clarity that always follows after it's expression, take whatever appropriate action there is to take.

Speaking of action, there's no time like the present, right? So, put this book or device down and take 60 seconds. Really, right now. Just put your hands on your heart, close your eyes, and breathe in your nose and out your mouth. Ask yourself, what am I actually feeling right now? If nothing comes to your awareness after 5 or 10 seconds, you can ask which of the following emotions you are most closely feeling (sadness, anger, happiness or fear). Okay, now set a timer on your digital device and go for it!

So, one of the things you may have noticed is that there is a strong tendency for our minds to weigh in and dominate the experience with all kinds of thoughts that have nothing to do with actually feeling anything. This is an important dynamic to be aware of as you begin to bring greater awareness to your emotions. For some people, it's helpful to return your awareness to the physical body for a few seconds first, before you begin becoming aware of the emotional content.

If you'd like, you can return to the previous exercise one more time with this new awareness about how the mind can suffocate the emotions.

Now it's time to dive into expanding mind awareness: a tricky proposition to be sure! Why? Well, because we are leveraging the same EM to be both the examiner and the examined. You may have noticed that as we move from body to emotions to mind, the volume of information and the complexity of that information increases. For the body, the messages are quite simple and basic. With emotions, we find that there is a broader range and that the richness of the experience of emotions makes the expanding awareness a far more colorful experience than simply tuning into the messages coming directly from the body alone.

Well, as we now enter the EM of the mind, the quantity of information to sift through reaches a fever pitch. As with both of the previous EMs we have explored expanding the awareness of, delving into the mind requires a particular kind of focus and ability to hone in. If you truly pay attention, you'll notice that your mind never really stops thinking. At any given moment, unless you happen to be in a state of transcendental bliss, there is a thought that you are thinking. It's happening when you are alone, when you're with others, when you're talking, and when you are silent. It's even happening when you're sleeping.

In order to expand awareness of this 3rd EM, you will want to discover what exactly these thoughts are. And once you know what they are, you can begin to assess which thoughts are empowering, disempowering, and neutral. I've created a simple exercise that will allow you to do just that. You'll set a timer on your digital device for 2 minutes. Then, you're simply going to write down whatever it is that you're thinking, non-stop. It does not at all matter what the content of your thoughts/writing is. What matters is that you are not filtering your thoughts but instead writing down exactly what your mind is entertaining over the course of the 2 minutes.

So, please put the book down, set the timer and get to it!

Welcome back! Okay, so now you've got these thoughts in place where we can interact with them. Next, I want you to rate each sentence or phrase you wrote. You can rate each sentence or phrase as either neutral (n), empowered (e), or disempowered (d). Don't get too hung up on any one sentence or phrase. When in doubt, label it as neutral. Once you are finished with that, simply add up the total for each.

What you now have is a simple snapshot of the landscape of your thoughts. So, what do you notice? Is there one kind of thought that is clearly outweighing the others or are they all quite even? Are you surprised by the relative amount of empowered or disempowered thoughts you're having?

When I do this exercise, it creates a few different opportunities. First, I am able to get my thoughts from inside my head out into the world and on paper where I can actually work with them. This simple move is extremely powerful, especially for those of us who tend to get lost in ourselves and in repetitive thought loops. Once I can see my thoughts on a piece of paper, I am no longer completely identified with them and can recognize them as the temporary things that they are. With practice, I can even begin to see that many of the thoughts I'm having are actually ones I've borrowed from someone else or the culture at large. When I see this, I'm free to switch thoughts to one that is empowered or neutral, rather than disempowered.

Secondly, by forcing myself to observe, in reality, how empowered or disempowered my thinking is, I have the opportunity for a reality check. For example, generally, when someone asks me how I'm doing, my response is something like "Really good!" However, if I were to run this exercise once per day and see that, in fact, 60% of my thinking is either neutral or disempowered, I know that I'm not exactly being honest with myself or with those around me. I then have the opportunity to dig deeper, ask for support or take some action to deal with the disempowered thoughts in a way that serves me.

Finally, the exercise is humbling. By writing down all that is running through my mind, I am able to find compassion for myself. We live incredibly complex and sometimes overwhelming internal lives. By taking a moment to get present to all that's going on, I find that I am able to approach myself and my day with a gentle sense of reverence and care.

You see, what we're interested in here is not only the actual thoughts you're having, but in what is the nature of the background approach or stance you have in relation to *whatever* it is you are thinking about. Forgetting the content of each and every thought, what is the context for your thinking? Do you have a bias toward disempowerment or empowerment? It almost doesn't matter what the subject is that you are having thoughts about. What's interesting is whether you have a general tendency to be empowered, disempowered, or neutral in your relationship to what you are thinking about. If you find that you are disempowered, you know that there is something out of whack with your EMs. And once you see that, you have access to shift from disempowered to empowered. Sometimes, this shift will require you to switch focus from the mind to one of the other EMs to get juiced up before diving back into what can sometimes be the dark forest of the mind.

Okay, so now we're ready to begin expanding your level of awareness of your higher self. As promised in Chapter 1, my intention is to offer even the most practically minded a way to access this virtually limitless source of energy. While I don't promise to know the ultimate truth about the nature of our higher self, I have had direct experience of being guided by something that I cannot consider to be my rational, thinking mind. In fact, this book project itself was born of an experience of connection to my higher self during a Kundalini yoga session. Whether or not our "higher self" represents our subconscious mind or our eternal soul is not as important as being able to have the experience of connecting to this source of energy that can quite literally "blow your mind."

To begin to engage with this EM, here is a simple exercise. Set up a comfortable space to sit in. Prior to sitting down, write down the following questions, leaving space in between them so that you can answer them during the exercise:

Higher Self Questions

○ Why have I been given this opportunity of a life?
○ Given the particular set of life circumstances that have molded me so far AND the skill sets that I have developed, what is a gift that I am uniquely qualified to offer to other human beings?
○ Imagine yourself in the few moments before dying. Look back on your life and locate yourself where you are now. What are the three most important things that happened between that moment (now) and the moment of your death?

You may find that, initially, your mind is resistant to this exercise. There is good reason for this resistance from the mind's perspective. You see, the mind's job is to help you figure things out, navigate life and deal with challenges and problems. It knows that as you get clearer about why you are here and what you have to offer, it's going to have less work to do. I encourage you to stick with the exercise until you can at least write one sentence in response to each of the three questions.

As you have experienced from having done the exercises, engaging with the different fundamental energy sources that are available to you requires you to apply your focused attention and awareness in a particular way. It is developing the skill set to do this, as and when needed, that provides you with an experience of being well-resourced and supported as you design and navigate a satisfied, empowered life.

Now that you've had a taste of cultivating awareness for each of the EMs, it's time to begin to do just that. In the next chapter we'll walk through the nuts and bolts of putting together your first personalized, satisfied life experiment.

CHAPTER 4

ONE WEEK SATISFACTION BOOSTER

t's now time to move from understanding to utilization, from philosophy to personalization. In this chapter, you are going to get clear about an area of life that you'll be focusing on, for the next week or so, in order to boost your overall level of life satisfaction. You'll then be rating the current health of your relationship with the EMs, both in general and in the specific area of life you're focused on. And finally, you will create a course of action to begin to leverage the EMs to impact both this specific area of life AND your overall level of life satisfaction.

In order to move from understanding to utilization, I'm including a worksheet to guide you as we walk through this chapter together.

Area of Life Satisfaction Ratings

Health/Well-Being:_____

Finances:_____

Intimate Relationship: _____

Career/Job:_____

Family Relationships: _____

Social Life/Friends: _____

Other (_____): _____

Life Overall: _____

Area of Life To Focus On: _____

Current Satisfaction Rating Specific To Area of Life (1-10): _____

Energy Magnifier Ratings (Generally, in Life)

Body: _____

Emotions: _____

Mind: _____

Self: _____

My Strongest EM Is: _____ My Weakest EM Is: _____

Energy Magnifier Ratings (Specific to The Area of Life I'm Focused on Increasing Satisfaction In)

Body: _____

Emotions: _____

Mind: _____

Self: _____

My Strongest EM Is: _____ My Weakest EM Is: _____

_____

Exercise I'm Going To Begin Experimenting With: _____

_____

Actions To Take (When Energy Becomes Available): _____

_____

_____

I've also included 10 additional worksheets at the end of the book for your use going forward.

So, let's begin with honing in on the area of life that you will be working with. You can assign a rating from 1-10 to the different areas of your life that are important to you. A rating of 1 would indicate that you could not be less satisfied with that area of your life and that very little, if anything, is working. And 10 would indicate that you can't even imagine that area of your life being any better than it already is because it's just that amazing.

Now, to help you get a head start on identifying all the areas of life there are to consider, I'll list them here. But, by no means should you let this list limit you. It's important that you give some thought to identifying all of the key areas of life that impact your overall experience of life and the degree to which you are satisfied with it.

- ○ Health/Well-Being
- ○ Finances
- ○ Intimate Relationship
- ○ Career/Job
- ○ Family Relationships
- ○ Social Life/Friends

And then, rate your overall level of life satisfaction from 1-10 as well.

Once you've got a rating for each of the areas, you have two choices. You can either simply choose the area of life with the lowest rating to focus on OR you can pause a moment and reflect on this question: "Which area of life, if I were to focus on it and boost the level of my satisfaction in that area, would have the greatest impact on my overall level of life satisfaction?"

So now that you've got an area of life to focus on, it's helpful to get a sense for which mode or modes you've been operating from lately relative to the Satisfaction Sustainability Matrix. Here it is again to refresh your memory:

Perhaps you've been completely unconscious in this area for the past few weeks/months/years. Perhaps you've been popping back and forth between unsustainable satisfaction and exploring satisfaction. Perhaps you've been operating in expanding

Satisfaction Sustainability Matrix

satisfaction mode. No matter how you've been operating, what's important is to see *how* you've been operating so that you are completely clear about your starting point.

Now we can begin delving into the EMs. What we want to determine here is how well you are currently leveraging each of the EMs. And, for each EM, there is a particular way to assess this, using a scale from 1-10.

Let's start with your body. If you look back at the past week, on any given day, what would be the average percentage of time that your body was either 1) in action mode, energized and in the flow or 2) on what I would call "potent standby"? By this, I mean, if you did require something of it, it would be able to provide it to you. For example, if you had to suddenly run to catch the bus, could you do that without injuring yourself?

What you are assessing here is what percentage of the time your body is in sufficiently good shape that you are able to engage with whatever activity you want to be engaged with or that you could if you wanted to.

When you have the percentage of time, you can then translate that into a number from 1-10. For example, if you've come up with 60%, that would correspond to 6 on a scale from 1-10. 50% would be 5. And so on.

Now that we've assessed body, let's move to your emotions. To arrive at a number from 1-10 here, you want to look at the percentage of the time that you are present to and honoring your emotional state. This *does not* mean that you are in a constant state of dramatic emotional expression. ☺ What it does mean is that you are aware of your emotional state and that you are honoring it. Honoring your emotional state can take many forms. Sometimes it means that you simply need to get present to an emotion and express it (sadness, anger, fear, etc.). Other times, it requires you to shift your behavior in some way (for example, if you are frustrated, it may require you to look at what led you to this moment so that you can make adjustments in your life that make it less likely you'll find yourself in that place again). And, sometimes, honoring your emotions means expressing those emotions to someone.

So, as you look at the past week, give yourself a rating of 1-10, for the percentage of time you are present to and honoring your emotional state.

On to the mind! Much like the exercise you did earlier where you wrote out your thoughts and then assessed them as to whether they were empowered, disempowered or neutral, when assessing the EM of mind, you are looking to see what percentage of the time your thoughts are empowered.

Empowered thoughts are those that bring energy and aliveness, and have you either present to what's working in life or energized to generate the changes needed to have your life working even better than it is now.

So, again here, from 1-10, assess yourself, on average over the past week.

And finally, it's time to assess your higher self. Now, this one gets a little squirrelly. You see, when we attempt to move beyond the mind, things like "amount of time" and "scale of 1-10" mean less. ☺ This is because our concept of time and numbers are inventions of the human mind. And so we'll take a different tactic here. What you want to assess is the degree to which you have the experience of what I describe as "dancing through life." In other words, do you have regular moments of awe at the way your life is unfolding? Do you regularly stop to appreciate the sheer beauty and magnificence of the natural world (a bird soaring through the sky, a sunset, a beautiful tree, the sun or a breeze on your face)? How often are you observing your thoughts rather than being at the mercy of them. Don't worry about getting this right. Just see if you can pick a number between 1 and 10 that represents the degree to which you know that, in reality, no matter what the particular circumstances of your life are, all is, truly, well. Write this number down. It will do for now.

Now that you've chosen an area of life to focus on and you have a general awareness of how engaged you currently are with each of the EMs, there's just one more assessment to make before you get into action. You now want to assess the EMs *specifically* in relationship to the area of life that you will be focusing on this week. For example, let's say that you have rated yourself at an 8 in life overall for the EM of body and you are focused on increasing your level of satisfaction in the specific area of work/career. What you now want to do is the same assessment, however, specific to your work life. So, what percentage of the time you are spending at work is your body in action/in the flow or in "potent standby" mode?

And then, you'll do the same for the other three EMs. What you will sometimes find is that there can be a difference between your overall ratings and your ratings for a particular area of life. This, in and of itself, can be illuminating as it can shine some light on why an area of your life may not be working so well, while most other areas of life are.

Okay, so now what? You've got an area of life to focus on and you've got your assessments for the EMs for both your life overall and this specific area. Now it's time to consciously engage the EMs. Again here, in much the same way as you did when choosing an area of life, it can be good to step back with the EMs and see whether it makes the most sense to directly engage with the EM that is rated lowest OR whether there is another EM that you sense would provide the biggest boost in satisfaction in the area of life you are focused on.

Whichever path you choose, you'll then want to determine which mode you're in (awareness/exploring satisfaction or committed action/expanding satisfaction). This is important because these two modes ask very different things of you. While both modes share the feature of small changes, awareness mode has a lot more to do with discovery whereas committed action has more to do with consistently applied action. These different modes will involve a different approach when it comes to what you'll actually be focused on over the next week. Most of the rest of the book features chapters dedicated to each of the pillars in both awareness and committed action mode.

Generally speaking, I recommend that you stick to awareness mode if your level of satisfaction in the area of life you're working with is less than a 6. If your level of satisfaction is low, consider that there is more to learn about your EMs in this area of life before you move into committed action mode.

Okay, so now let's get into action! Turn to the chapter that is relevant to the mode and EM you are working with, read it completely, and then choose from one of the exercises/practices in the chapter. In my experience, when you're in awareness mode, it's advisable to start off with just one exercise in the beginning and work with that for 2 or 3 days before considering adding an additional one. If you are in committed action mode and you're feeling frisky, you can consider kicking things off with 2 practices from the get go.

There is one last critical piece to this process. Be on the lookout for an increase in your level of energy/excitement/clarity in the area of your life you are focused on as you begin to work with the EM you've chosen. As you begin to notice this boost, it's essential that you channel that energy into some kind of conscious shift in how you're operating. This can be scheduling a conversation with someone to share what you are uncovering. Or, it could be that you take some kind of action in the area of your life you're focused on. For example, if you were focused on the area of intimate relationship, you might head out to a new social gathering that you have been meaning to check out. The idea here is to "strike while the iron is hot" as they say. It may also look like taking a look at the remainder of your week in your calendar and moving things around or putting events in that increase the likelihood that you'll experience the shift you're looking to see in your level of satisfaction in that area of life.

Remember, especially if you are in awareness mode, this process will include some learning and may require some adjusting as you go. It may be that the exercise you chose wasn't the best one for your unique mental/emotional/physical/spiritual make-up. It may also be that "life happens" and you get sidetracked with the exercise(s) for a day or two. This is normal, and even likely to happen, in my experience working with people. But here's my promise to you: If you actively engage with this work over the course of a week, you will realize a significant shift in the area of life you are focused on. The EMs are simply too powerful to be denied.

Later in the book, I'll be sharing with you the best tips and tricks that I've accumulated over the last 10 years to keep you motivated, on track and moving forward toward your life satisfaction goals.

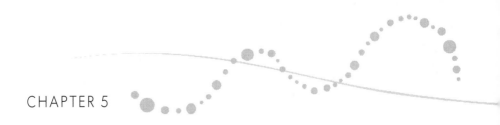

CHAPTER 5

Let's Get Physical

When we look closely at the natural world, the basic requirement for physical restoration and renewal for all living things is apparent. Everything from a dog nibbling for ticks to a hibernating bear reminds us that there must be a time when we are called to turn inward, tending to our immediate physical needs. Almost all of us understand that this requirement applies to us as human beings as well. We brush our teeth every day and at least make an effort to eat foods that we know are not going to significantly negatively impact our overall health. We know the importance of getting our bodies moving each day and may even indulge in some pampering in the form of a massage or some time in the sauna now and then.

You are reading this chapter because you have determined that you would like to deepen or strengthen your connection to this Energy Magnifier. One of the ways to do that is to become aware of your blind spots in this area. This chapter outlines the full range of opportunities to engage with the EM of the body. And, more than that, it offers you specific tools to do so, with the aim of fully connecting to this incredible resource.

There are three smaller magnifiers – what you're putting in your body, what you're doing with your body and how you're caring for your body - that make up the overall magnifier of the body. Engaging with any one of them will boost your level of body energy available. Engaging with all three will positively turbo-charge you. Let's look first at the area of what's going in to your body.

What's Going In?

If you step back and consider it, what is your body actually composed of? When the cells of your skin, blood, brain and stomach wear out and need to be replaced, what does your DNA use to make new cells? Well, there's only thing it can use and that's whatever you are giving it! And so, it's critical that you bring your attention to what is going in.

Now, this didn't used to be a major concern when human beings were hunter-gatherers. While we certainly had an opportunity to go out of balance with our nutritional needs from time to time, we were not nearly so separate from where our food came from and how it was made. For our ancestors, not a day went by when they weren't intimately engaged with foraging, hunting, grinding, crushing or baking their food.

Of course, now, you can walk into a supermarket and look around to find that more than 80% of what you see is not in a form that a human being could make on their own. I like to call these products "food-like substances." And, as you may know, the corporations manufacturing these substances are primarily motivated by one outcome and that is profit. Why can I say this with such certainty? Well, I worked in the business world for over a decade and I didn't meet one fellow businessperson during that entire time that was working for a company that wasn't focused, every day, on their bottom line. Now don't get me wrong. The food manufacturers are not likely to be the devil incarnate. However, you are being naive if you think they have your best health interests as their primary concern when they go to sleep at night.

This book cannot (nor, could any book, really) tell you exactly what you need to be putting into your body every day, week, month or year of your life. What I can say with absolute certainty is that it's important that you pay attention to what you are putting in there. It seems to me there are **three critical questions** to ask yourself on an ongoing basis in this regard:

- ○ Have you drunk a sufficient amount of water? I actually use the urine test. If it's more than a little yellow, I know I need some more.
- ○ How much of the food that you've eaten in the last day or week has been something a human being could have created on their own, in their own kitchen?
- ○ Is there some symptom going on in your body right now and, if so, can you trace it to something you've put in your body in the last 24 hours or so?

This last one deserves a bit more explanation, huh? What I'm *not* suggesting is that absolutely every symptom your body displays is the direct result of a food you have recently eaten. What I *am* saying is that, often, I've noticed that a symptom my body is displaying can be traced to a food I've overindulged in or is missing from my diet. For example, when I eat more than a serving or two of cheese in a given two- or three-day time frame, I'm prone to have a stuffy nose. And if I keep eating cheese and/or eat something else that my body has a relatively low tolerance for, I up my chance for catching a full on cold.

I want to emphasize that I'm not saying you will have this same reaction. I am saying that you have your version of this phenomenon. It could be related to gluten, or sugar, or even bananas for all I know! The important thing to get is that your body responds to what you are putting into it and the more you are aware of the responses, the greater the connection you will have to the energy magnifier that is your body.

You see your body naturally generates energy. Have you noticed that, even without paying too much attention to it, your body will turn food into energy for you? Even if you feed it things it really doesn't want, it will still give you the energy to get through a typical day. But when you give it the things that are optimal for its functioning, it provides an abundance of energy to power you even on the most challenging of days.

Is It Strong & Supple?

Ah, exercise. What is it about moving our bodies and increasing our heart rate that confronts so many of us? I know some highly active and trained athletes that still encounter resistance getting up in the morning to go for a run. One theory postulates that the near universality of this challenge is partly due to the fact that the only other time when we need to get our heart rate up and work our muscles to this extent is when we're having a fight or flight response. And, really, why would anyone consciously create that body/emotional state if there were no imminent danger?

So, unless you've already managed to short circuit this primal connection by associating exercise with some positive outcome (for example the pride of having beaten your personal best running time or finally getting into that pretzel-like yoga pose) it's going to take something specific to get you motivated. If you're one of those people who hasn't yet made friends with exercise, I'm going to attempt to inspire you here.

I want you to imagine yourself approaching a young girl or boy of 8 or 9 one afternoon at the playground. Imagine that you are somehow able to get their attention for a minute or two between games of hide-and-seek and crawling all over the jungle gym. Now, I want you to ask the child this very simple question, "At what age do you want to stop being able to run around and play like you're doing now?" Now, immediately imagine yourself at their age, and picture yourself playing with them. How would you have answered the question when you were their age?

You see there is no answer to that question, really. No one who knows what it's like to be able to run and jump and lift things and build things and dance wildly would imagine a day when they wouldn't want to at least have the option to do that. So, each time you are considering whether to exercise or not, you really just have to ask yourself two questions:

- ○ Will this activity allow me to be even more capable and free to use my body to enjoy life fully?
- ○ Will this activity actually have me enjoying life more fully in that moment?

I have just one final thought on exercise. If you have not yet truly considered all that a strong, supple body makes possible in your life, I recommend you take a few minutes, right now, and fill a page or two from the heart of your inner child. What would that 8- or 9-year-old have wished for you at the age you're at now? What would they have said about how they would be using their body later in life? What experiences did they want to have?

Are You Loving It Up?

Many people, even if they are paying attention to what they are taking in and what they are doing to keep their body strong and supple, look at me like I've got three heads when I ask them what actions they take to demonstrate their love and appreciation for their body. And I kind of get it. Whether it's commitments to family or work or just a long running familial or cultural story that tells us that pampering ourselves is a luxury we cannot afford, we have no shortage of barriers to taking the time to give to our bodies in this way.

Just as what we put in and what we do with our bodies is highly individual, the same goes for how we choose to care for our body. A warm bubble bath can be the answer for one person and be someone else's worst nightmare. That said, there are some core principles to be guided by and some key indicators for when it's time to pay more attention in this way.

The first core principle is rest. I'm not talking only about the infamous 8 hours of sleep that we're all "supposed" to get. In fact, studying human history and even current reality, ample evidence suggests that one long sleep per 24-hour cycle is not necessarily the optimal pattern. I'm talking here about the full range of rest from deep sleep to afternoon siestas to 5 minutes just simply closing your eyes and allowing your breathing to equalize in a quiet environment.

When you rest your body, and particularly your nervous system, you turn the volume down on the somatic nervous system and give the autonomic nervous system a chance to be addressed. You move from action/external awareness to repair/rejuvenate mode. This is not just a concept. There is a physical, biological shift in how your body is operating when you close down your senses.

I've learned about and experienced first-hand the value of consciously addressing both the somatic and autonomic systems from many different wisdom traditions including chiropractic and Kundalini yoga.

Many people in the medical field chime in on this subject. Dr. Dan Siegel talks about "brain nutrition." Remember, in addition to being the place where all your thoughts are formed (we'll be delving into that realm a bit later), our brain is also a physical part of our bodies. Years of brain research helped him and his colleague David Rock distinguish the importance of having downtime to allow the brain to just be, with nothing in particular to focus on.

Physical trainers and Olympic athlete coaches also emphasize the importance of rest. They know that, in reality, the results of any work out we complete are never actually happening while we're working out. It's only when we are resting that the body can fully focus on repairing tissue damage, replenishing our hormonal reserves and optimizing our circulatory and nervous systems to handle that next challenge.

The second core principle is attention to breath. Simply put, the quality of your breathing has a massive impact on your capacity to be engaged, energized and aware. It is nearly impossible for you to experience being "stressed out" when you are consciously bringing your attention to the inhalation and exhalation of your breath. Rather than talking at length about the power of attention to breath to create the experience of what I call an "energized calm", I invite you to experience this right now, in your body.

Here's how you're going to do this. Simply read until the end of this paragraph and then immediately put the book/tablet down and get to it. This exercise will work no matter where you are (train, airport or curled up on your couch). First, set a timer on your digital device for 2 minutes. Then, put the palms of your hands on your thighs and close your eyes. Simply observe the inhale and exhale of your breath. There are only two things to be aware of. First, notice that, without any effort at all from you, your breathing is always happening. When you get present to this, something shifts in your awareness that is hard to describe yet shifts your state to one of calm. Second, once you are focusing on the breath, bring your attention to the length of inhale and exhale. Your aim, during the two minutes, is to move towards bringing the inhale and exhale to the same length of time. Start with shortening the longer one to the length of the shorter one and then, if you like, stretch them both out equally. For example, if your inhale is 8 seconds and your exhale is 3, bring your inhale down to 3 and then expand both to 5 and then to 7, etc. I suggest you re-read this paragraph one more time and then put the book/device down and get to it!

Welcome back! What you've just done has had so many positive impacts on your body. For thousands of years, those who were concerned with maximizing their level of consciousness and presence in order to live the most fulfilling life possible have known about the importance of breath awareness. You've now had a small taste of what's possible.

The third core principle is to minimize the bacterial and chemical stress on the body. Your body is constantly defending against viruses, bacteria and chemicals from the environment that have no business being there. This job falls to the immune and lymphatic systems. Of course, it begins with paying attention to your home environment, with particular attention to the products that you are putting on your body and the foods you are putting in. One rule of thumb that I use when it comes to putting something on my body on a consistent basis is that I either use products that clearly describe the origin of the ingredients used or I ensure that I am clear that certain known ingredients (parabens, phthalates, BHA, etc.) are not present. Another piece of awareness is to consider what cleaning fluids you are using for your dishes, floors and windows. I like to use products that have as small a number of ingredients as possible and that have more natural ingredients. Of course, it's not likely that any one particular product would have the capacity to overwhelm your formidable immune defenses, however, the cumulative effect of multiple products over multiple years, both ingested and topically, certainly could. There are many other suggested ways for you to support both your immune and lymphatic systems, which you can find in the resources chapter of this book.

The fourth and final principle is one of luxuriating. While similar to rest, this principle involves the unabashed giving to yourself of special attention that just plain feels good. While sleeping or napping generally feels good after it's happened, you're not actually conscious during it. When you are luxuriating, you are enjoying every last second of it. Why is this so important? Well, the way I see it, we were born with whatever chemical receptors are necessary to allow us to feel the sweet sensations that course through our nervous system when we receive a massage, take a long bath or enjoy a facial or some other kind of skin treatment. And what people often notice is that even a 15- or 20-minute investment in pure enjoyment during their day makes the rest of what you have to deal with and handle much more manageable.

Perhaps most importantly, when you spend the time luxuriating, you learn a lot about your particular body's needs. Specifically, you learn what level of self care is required for you to be able to deal effectively with your life and everything in it with a minimum of the stress response that so many of us believe is just "how it is" these days. And I know that it can seem like luxuriating can be just another thing to 'squeeze in' to your day. But I invite you to consider that there are some activities that you engage in that are net energy spenders (crawling around on the internet or watching that second episode of your current TV show obsession) and some that are net energy magnifiers. Luxuriating fits squarely in that second camp.

Body Awareness Exercises

If you've made it this far through the chapter, I am assuming you have already completed your one week satisfaction booster worksheet from Chapter 4. If not, I recommend you head on over there before continuing so that you have the full context for what these exercises are about.

The tools highlighted here have been chosen specifically for their capacity to increase your level of body awareness. Some of them act as physical rejuvenators for when you're just about to reach (or have already reached) your physical capacity to "just keep going." They are designed to fortify and strengthen your body and address any barriers to your body's natural tendency to heal itself.

Others are more exploratory in nature, giving you the opportunity to expand your awareness of (or step back and get some perspective on) the current state of your body.

All of them are designed to take 10 minutes or less, and most of them can be completed in less than 5 minutes. It's important, especially as you begin to engage with increasing your level of body awareness, to start simply. What I've found in working with people is that the most impactful and sustainable shifts in life satisfaction occur when one can identify multiple opportunities throughout the day to initiate simple and swift shifts in focus or interrupt the existing behavior pattern *in the moment when it's most called for*.

It's one thing to look back on the day and bring awareness to the different times when it would have been useful to tune into the Energy Magnifier of the body. It's another thing to have actually done something differently a few times and realized the material benefit of having done so.

What follows are a group of exercises to choose from. As discussed in earlier chapters, it's usually best to begin with engaging with just one for a few days before attempting to take on another. We want to avoid overwhelm as well as give your body-mind a chance to register the impacts of one before adding in another.

I have consciously included a broad range of exercises for two different types of people. First, there are some people who just generally do best increasing their level of awareness or engaging with an activity if they have someone else to come along for the ride with them. So, I've included exercises that either require or offer that option. And then, there are exercises that are designed to be done with oneself, for those who do best relating with themselves first before interacting with others.

In my experience, different people "process" information in different ways. You may be aware of the many different models out there that categorize people according to their learning style. Perhaps you've heard terms like "visual learner, auditory learner, or kinesthetic learner," which are used in the field of Neuro-linguistic Programming. For the purposes of this book and particularly for the one week life satisfaction boost, just be aware of your preferred method for receiving and integrating new information and experiences. While it's likely that you will subconsciously choose exercises based on your preferred learning style, it's also possible that you'll choose an exercise that is not best suited for how you learn. **For this reason, I recommend that, if after a day or two, you are not clearly expanding your level of awareness, then change the exercise that you are engaging with.**

That said, this does not mean you should change up the exercise if it makes you uncomfortable or if you see something during the exercise that you don't like. ☺ In fact, seeing something that makes you uncomfortable and beginning to deal with that discomfort can be incredibly valuable for your growth and evolution.

Just one note to keep in mind about how the Energy Magnifiers work. While this chapter and these particular exercises are clearly aimed at impacting the body directly, many exercises featured in this book can and will impact multiple magnifiers.

And so, without further ado, let's dive into the exercises! Your best bet is to read through them all before settling on the one you're going to try first. We are all unique and these exercises are designed to be effective for a wide variety of learning styles and personality types.

Mini Cardio and/or Strength Building Break

I first experienced the benefits of this exercise while working at a start up online media company in New York City. A few times a week, one of the account executives (David Kert) and I would stop by each other's desks and invite the other to a quick push-up session. We'd find ourselves an empty conference room, choose the number of sets and repetitions of push-ups we were going to do, and then we'd go for it. The whole thing from deciding to do it to washing my hands afterward was never more than 5 minutes, which was shorter than the cigarette break some of my other co-workers would take!

Beyond the noticeable toning and bulking in my upper chest and back, there was the benefit of increased blood flow to my brain and the capacity to return to my desk with fresh eyes to survey what would be the best use of my time for the remainder of the morning, afternoon, or evening.

If you want to get more creative, you could stash a couple of light weights under your desk to work with specific muscle groups or even grab a buddy to hold your feet down as you do some sit-ups. Of course, you could also do these exercises on your own if you've got that level of discipline. When it comes to the sit-ups, you'd need to locate a place to tuck your feet under.

The primary intention here is simply to engage with the EM of body. This exercise is not intended to be a substitution for a fully realized workout plan. And, of course, before engaging with any strenuous exercise, it is always a good idea to do what you need to do to ensure that you are in sufficient health to engage with it. This may include consulting your health professional.

Deepening The Breath

Perhaps the exercise that requires the least effort in this entire book is the one I'm about to describe. You don't need any props, or anyone else, or even to use any muscles (except your diaphragm). Set the timer on your smart-phone or watch for between 2 and 5 minutes. Then, simply close your eyes and begin paying attention to your breathing. You'll breathe in for 5 seconds, hold your breath in for 5 seconds, breathe out for 5 seconds and hold your breath out for 5 seconds. And, that's it! Some people find it helpful to visualize a relaxing place or even to repeat a word for every second that passes (such as calm, God or love). I recommend to start with 2 minutes and then build your way up to 5 or more.

Besides giving the body a chance to bathe in oxygen rich blood, you're also giving your mind a mini-break as you focus in on the counting and a single word rather than the endless train of thoughts and reactions we're typically having.

Mini-Massage

When you think about it, you are a walking massage waiting to happen. The two critical elements (a body and two hands) are with you wherever you go! In fact, I see many people unconsciously massage their neck or lower back from time to time. The benefits of massage are many and varied according to numerous studies. They include boosting immunity, easing pain, reducing stress levels and improving sleep.

You can choose from focusing in on a particular stress area like the neck or give yourself a general full body massage, starting with the extremities and heading in to the center of the body. You don't even have to take your shoes off, although it certainly does feel nice. Head to the Resources section at the end of the book for a link to a "How To" on self-massage.

You can spend as little or as much time as you want. Some people find that a longer one at a particular, critical time of day is best, while others go with more frequent, shorter ones. And, if you are comfortable with physical contact with someone that's often around you, you can give this gift to each other.

Somato Respiratory Integration (SRI™) Exercise

SRI is a modality that I have personally practiced for nearly 10 years. Created by Dr. Donald Epstein, it's a powerful, self-directed tool that I use regularly to unlock hidden energetic resources. It involves placing the hands on certain parts of the body and focusing attention using awareness of not only the breath, but also the movement of the body *and* becoming aware of the feeling or "energy" present in different parts of the body.

Because most SRI exercises require your coordinated attention to breath, movement and energy and multiple positions on the body, I've created an audio file that will guide you through the experience. Simply head over to "www.consciousliving.ning.com" to register to join the community for readers of the book and there you'll find a forum which includes the audio file of the SRI exercise.

Stretching or Mini Yoga Set

You've seen it thousands of times. Someone is working hard at their computer or has just woken up from a nap or a long spell of sitting and they stretch their arms over their heads and/or stretch their legs and feet. In that moment, the body is getting a little taste of what it needs to keep the blood flow strong and rinse out the muscles of any unnecessary metabolic byproducts that may be accumulating. You can take this further by carving out a few minutes to stretch some of the major muscle groups.

It's as easy as 1-2-3…4-5. For each of these exercises, just spend 20-30 seconds. First, stand with your hands on your hips and move your pelvis in the clockwise direction and then in the opposite direction. Then, bend forward and place your hands on either your knees, shins or feet. Next, stand back up and gently stretch your neck by spinning your head clockwise and then counter-clockwise. After that, stretch your left fingertips up to the sky and bend over toward your right and then the same thing with the other side. Finally, clasp your hands behind your back and stretch them upwards while lifting your chest.

Skincare 2.0

During my own personal journey toward balanced health and well-being, I've heard many suggestions around taking care of the skin. And I'm talking about skincare beyond a simple moisturizer. Whether it's a gentle oil massage, a hot towel scrub or a cold shower, the act of attending to our largest organ delivers many and varied benefits. You can make taking care of your body in this way a special treat before or after a bath or incorporate a practice into your daily shower routine. It's about tuning in to what your body needs.

One of the great side effects of any of these practices is that they force you to really get present to your body rather than just being focused on keeping it clean. There is a practical benefit to this as well as you can check the health of your skin and have a look around for anything out of the ordinary (rashes, dry spots, sun spots, etc.).

I think this attention has an emotional side effect as well. Engaging in this way with your body is an expression of the appreciation and love you have for both it and you. As well, you can positively influence your mental state. The body and the mind, while different in their function, are both parts of the broader you and wherever you positively impact one, you can't help but influence the other as well.

For more specific instruction on cold showering or hot towel scrubs, flip to the references and resources chapter at the end of the book.

Monitoring Your "Inbox"

Less of a specific exercise and more of a mini-health boost, one way to engage with and fortify the EM of the body is to layer in some simple, yet powerful, health fortifying behaviors into your day. You can choose from the following list and, if you like, add one suggestion on the first day of the week, another on the third or fourth day and another on the fifth or sixth.

- ○ Drink a 16 oz. glass of lemon water first thing upon waking and another 16 oz. glass of water when the sun goes down.
- ○ Buy a 5-6 oz. pre-washed bag of some kind of dark leafy green (spinach, romaine, arugula, etc.) every two days and finish it by the time you buy the next one.

○ Have one meal of your day be completely un-processed, meaning that all of the ingredients are either in their natural form or could be easily made by a human being. So, yes, you can include something like olive oil or lemon juice on a salad. And, yes, you can use a machine to make a smoothie. And sure, you can put some butter on that sweet potato. ☺

○ For at least one meal per day, ensure that you are chewing each bite 20 times. Initially, it can be helpful to put the utensil you are using down between each bite to ensure you remember to chew.

With all of these suggestions, you'll notice that this is about adding in or being more mindful, not taking anything away. You may want to set a reminder in your digital device or place a Post-it® note on the handle of your refrigerator to help you get into the habit.

While these behaviors are simple, don't underestimate the impact they can have. Part of why they work so well is the concept of "crowding out," one of my very favorite principles from my training at the Institute for Integrative Nutrition®. As you focus on adding things in to your diet or behaviors into your day, you are bringing a new level of conscious awareness and avoiding unconscious, auto-pilot behaviors which are often neutral at best and often detrimental.

Self-Healing

Before we dive into this final exercise, I want to emphasize that neither this nor any of the exercises in this book are meant to replace or be a substitute for your relationship with a medical professional.

This exercise can be a profoundly eye-opening one, if you allow yourself to fully engage with it. At its core is one key concept, which is that while our body is a single entity, it is almost always exhibiting different states at the same time. For example, one part of your body may be deeply connected to peace and you can experience that when you place your hands there. Another part of your body may be exhibiting some kind of symptom (pain, tension, tightness, soreness, etc.). And another part of your body, when you place your hands there, can be a source of energy and vibrancy.

When you couple this reality with the fact that we can only really be present with one experience at a time, you have the ingredients for a powerful exercise.

The following words represent the way I engage with myself having learned of and experienced an exercise taught by Donny Epstein.

So, here's how it goes. For this exercise we're going to concern ourselves with two different embodied experiences. One is peace and the other is symptom. To begin, either lie down or sit comfortably in a chair. Close your eyes and focus your attention on the actual experience of being at peace. Sometimes it's helpful to visualize a peaceful scene or just remember the last time you were feeling completely at ease in your body. Then, see if you can sense for where in your body is a place that is particularly peaceful or where peace seems to be emanating from. When you can identify that place, bring your hands there and place them one on top of the other. For the next 45 seconds or so, continue focusing all of your attention on this part of your body as you breathe in and out and expand and contract this part of your body. Finally, and importantly, allow a sound to escape your lips on the exhale that reflects how you feel. This might be a gentle sigh or even something akin to a yogic "Aum."

Now, move you hand to any part of your body that is currently exhibiting some kind of symptom (pain, tension, tightness, soreness, etc.). Again, focus all your attention here, breathing in and out and expanding and contracting. Also here, allow a sound that reflects what you actually feel like when you focus on this part of your body. This might be a growl, moan or whimper. Here, you'll spend less time...20 seconds or so. Then head back to the place of peace and spend another 45 seconds there and then one more time to the place of symptom. When you arrive back at the place of symptom, when you exhale and make the sound, see if you can incorporate some of the sound from the peaceful place in this place of symptom. You may need to return back to the peaceful place a couple more times before you begin to notice the shift in the place of symptom.

The full power of this exercise lies in your ability to remain present with the two different experiences, letting your nervous system leverage the increased amount of time with the peaceful experience to permeate the time you are spending with the symptom.

And, the more you can allow yourself to make the true sound in each place, the more information your nervous system has to work with.

Remember, these exercises are my best suggestions for dealing directly with the energetic magnifiers. You are welcome to leverage exercises or modalities that you are already familiar with, search out new ones or create your own! For the most up-to-date thinking on all of these exercises and to share your experience or get support, you can head over to www.consciousliving.ning.com and register for access to the online community.

If you're anything like me, any one of these exercises, if it's the right one for you at this moment in time, can be surprisingly energizing and illuminating. As you walk further along this journey of engaging with the Energy Magnifier of the body, you may find that the exercises which make the most sense for you will change. And further, if you stick with this exploration long enough, you will soon find that you are inventing your very own practices for increasing your awareness! On behalf of your body, I invite you into a lifelong exploration of the ever-changing relationship between your awareness and the miracle that is your body.

CHAPTER 6

THE OCEAN OF EMOTION

Trying to control our emotions is like trying to control the weather. And yet, all of us, to varying degrees, attempt to do just that. We often find ourselves editing or delaying the expression of our emotions based on the situation we're in or based on a fear of what others may do or say in response to those emotions. This fear stems from early childhood experiences that taught us that full emotional expression made the adults around us, upon whom we depended on for survival, uncomfortable.

While this strategy may have some short-term benefit, longer term we cut ourselves off from an incredibly powerful energy source when we habitually mute or turn the volume down on the full range and depth of our emotions. In addition to being an energy source, our emotions are powerful and sometimes mysterious messengers that can lead us to profound growth and healing, if we give them the space to do so.

I can remember a period of time in my mid 20's when I would quite unexpectedly start crying during movies. I have several vivid memories of having to pause the movie I was watching in order to experience the full force of the sadness. Initially, my conscious mind was just kind of stunned at what was happening. But slowly, I began to realize that I was experiencing some of the sadness related to my father's death 15 years before. Over time, allowing myself the freedom to express these strangely intense emotions, left me in a more receptive mode when various methodologies and resources crossed my path that had the capacity to help me heal from this old wound.

Many times, what we're feeling "makes sense" based on the

situation; the intensity and type of emotion is a match for what's happening. In these cases, emotions are simply a way for our body-mind to connect with both the situation and the other people in it.

Then there are times when our emotions are either muted relative to the situation or vastly exaggerated relative to what's actually happening. You've seen this, I'm sure, with yourself or others. You may have had a sense of numbness even though the situation was quite intense or had someone tell you that you're "not getting them." Or maybe you've watched as a two people were having an argument in public and one of the two is going on and on in a colorful and intense way about some rather insignificant behavior that the other had exhibited.

When either of these two situations occur for us, or those we are interacting with, we have a particularly valuable opportunity to learn something new about ourselves and uncover some of our emotional blind spots. Later in this chapter, you'll be able to choose from a group of exercises that will assist you in getting to better know the map of your emotional landscape.

Another phenomenon that I've noticed (both with myself and those that I've worked with), regarding emotions, is the relentless tendency for the mind to insert itself into the realm of our emotions. And the thing is, its just doing its job, which is to attempt to interpret and come up with all kinds of rationale about why something is happening. While this is very useful in dealing with some of the complexities of life, when it comes to the emotions, it can have the effect of blunting the actual experience of the emotion, robbing us of that valuable energy source.

You see, the mind is not interested in you fully experiencing your emotions because it knows that the signals you are getting from the emotional realm may mean that life is going to have to change in some significant way, and the mind would rather keep the status quo and manage things just the way they are.

But what if we could develop new and powerful ways of both connecting to our emotions and communicating them? If we could, we could begin to shift how life unfolds around us, in our relationships, and in all the important areas of our life. It's possible for anyone who is willing to bring a new kind of awareness to his or her emotions and there are four core competencies that must be understood and practiced in order for it to happen.

The 4 Core Competencies of Emotional Connection

I've been able to distinguish four distinct aspects of what I call "emotional fluency." Before we dig into these competencies, let's answer the question of why we want to be fluent emotionally.

Simply put, emotional fluency, in addition to giving you access to all of what the EM of the emotions has to offer, increases your capacity to connect to more of yourself and also with other people. When you can express yourself emotionally with other people, there is a "realness" and an authenticity that is highly engaging. Those around you are able to recognize, sometimes only on a sub-conscious level, that the act of you expressing your emotions demonstrates that you are willing to expose yourself and be vulnerable. This realness and authenticity fosters trust, respect, and intimacy.

Vulnerability is on display even when so-called "negative" emotions like anger are being shown. Although anger is not always pleasant to be on the receiving end of, it's expression does demonstrate that the person being angry with you cares enough about you to express that emotion even though they run the risk of you choosing to no longer spend as much (or any) time around them. If you can see someone's expression of anger in this way, you may be able to return yourself to a state of compassion in dealing with him or her.

Thoughts vs. Emotions

The first aspect of emotional fluency involves being able to distinguish clearly, in your own mind and in your speaking, the difference between what you are feeling and what you are thinking. Many of us, most of the time, collapse our thoughts and our emotions into one. When we do this, we lose clarity of thought and we lose the potency of the emotional energy.

For example, you walk into your house or apartment after an extra long day at work. That morning, you had specifically asked your partner to clear out one of the rooms in your living space and they haven't. After realizing this, as they walk out of the bathroom, you hit them with the following: "I can't believe you didn't clean up the room! Why don't you ever listen to me?"

What's happening here is that the frustration and anger (emotions) that you are feeling are getting all tied up with a thought

("My partner is selfish" or "My partner doesn't care about me").
And this happens multiple times per day in more or less dramatic
ways. Oftentimes, it only happens in our mind and doesn't make it
into our communication but the impact is similar: a lack of clarity
and a loss of emotional potency.

How does this impact you in concrete terms? Well, in this
example, if you were able to distinguish your emotions from your
thoughts about what happened before you said what you said to
your partner, you might be able to see that your thought about your
partner not caring about you or being selfish stems from another
thought, which is that they are not supporting you in your growth
and evolution. How? Because you might realize that you had the
intention to use the cleared out space to start up a yoga practice.
And then you might see that you actually hadn't taken the time
this morning to share with them about this desire, and even more
importantly, your desire for them to support you in it.

If you had shared the reasoning as to why you wanted that
space cleared, they may have acted differently out of their love
and support for you. This alone can teach you a new approach for
the future that could be more effective. So, you might hold your
tongue that night and try talking with your partner about why it's
so important to you.

You can see how distinguishing thoughts from emotions leads
you to new conversations that are focused on what's actually
important (your level of support for one another's growth in this
case) rather than a specific behavior that did or didn't happen
(cleaning out the spare room). That behavior (or lack of behavior)
is simply the symptom, not the cause, of the emotional/mental
conflict.

Now that you've begun to see the benefits of distinguishing
your thoughts from your emotions, let's take a deeper dive into the
emotions themselves.

Owning Our Emotions (Especially the Reactive Ones)

Using the same example we can take a look at the second aspect of
emotional fluency, which is the capacity to own and be responsible
for all of our emotions, even those ones that seem to be so obviously
a direct result of what someone else has done. If you refer to what

was said in the example we've been using, everything that was said was in terms of the other person rather than in terms of the thoughts and emotions of the person who was upset. And so, instead of clear communication about what's going on, the person who is upset is in attack mode. I'm guessing you can recognize this pattern.

Only when you can own your reactions as your own, do you then have the capacity to connect with someone else. Consider that any emotional reaction you have was already there, loaded and ready to go, before whatever happened, happened. So the emotion is yours, and is simply being triggered by someone else. They are not the source of the emotion. The emotion exists within and is expressed by you. These emotional reactions are almost always safety mechanisms to protect us from feeling something that we don't want to feel.

When you are in an emotionally reactive state, there is very little space to connect with someone else. When we're in a reaction, we aren't able to just simply be with the other person and are instead fully in our own experience. When two people are in this state at the same time, there is no connection possible. And so, how can we create the conditions that foster connection to our own emotional state so that we can then increase our capacity to be with others' emotional states?

The best way that I have found to increase my capacity to be with emotions (both my own and others') is to practice experiencing my emotions on my own with no one else to bounce them off of. While this may seem simple and rudimentary in concept, it can be incredibly powerful in practice. Generally, we each have a set range of emotion that we are comfortable feeling on our own and another set that we are comfortable expressing with others. Each of us has certain emotions that we can more fully feel when we have someone else to react to. And so, allowing ourselves to feel certain emotions and stir them on our own can be quite challenging for some of us. In fact, for some people, the idea of feeling, let alone expressing, their emotions with no one else around seems downright odd! If this describes you, you're likely in for a big "aha" during the next exercise.

So, I'm inviting you to a 24-hour emotional awareness expanding exercise. This exercise will last from the moment you put this book down today until the same time tomorrow.

Here's how it goes: You're going to write down the following emotions along the left hand side of a sheet of paper (which we'll call the Emotional Tracker): joy, fear, sadness, and anger. Then, *every two hours* (you may want to set reminders on your phone and/or computer calendar now), you'll record 4 things. Use pencil, so you can erase and re-write the numbers every two hours.

1 Record the number of times you felt the emotion when you were by yourself and

2 (in parentheses) the number of times you actively expressed it (for example, cursing and slamming your hand down on your desk or huffing air out your nose or mouth to express anger or dancing around your home or smiling to express joy).

3 Record the number of times you felt the emotion while with other people and

4 (in parentheses) the number of times you expressed it in the presence of other people.

Regarding fear, the expression of this emotion can sometimes be less obvious. It can sometimes look like being immobilized for a period of time and/or taking some kind of frantic action to deal with the fear. Often it looks like some kind of repetitive thought pattern. As the exercise continues, you'll get sensitized to how it manifests in you.

When the 24 hours are up, your page would look something like this:

Joy	7 (3)	4 (3)
Fear	6 (1)	9 (2)
Sadness	4 (2)	2(0)
Anger	6 (3)	5 (4)

There's just one last thing to do before embarking on this experiment. On the other side of the sheet of paper, make your predictions as to how it's all going to turn out. Predict the number of times, in an average day, you will feel all the emotions, with yourself and with others, and the amount of times you'll express what you're feeling.

And that's it! If you're going to take this experiment on, I invite you to place this book down and not pick it up again until this time tomorrow. Deal?

. . . . . .

No peeking! Go and live your life and come back tomorrow! ☺

All right, welcome back! So, what have you learned? How were your prediction skills? Were you surprised by the number of times you felt emotions? Which of your emotions are you most likely to express with others? Which with yourself? Where did you experience the largest difference between the number of times feeling an emotion and the number of times actually expressing it?

You could be any number of places along the range of frequency with regard to feeling emotions. You may have experienced a relatively small number of emotions in the past 24 hours. This may simply have been the result of a relatively tranquil period of time in your life. You may also be someone who has historically been able to suppress or avoid your emotions such that your level of sensitivity to them is not very high. Or, conversely, it may have been a particularly intense period and your numbers were very high. Wherever you are is completely fine. The point is not to reduce or increase the frequency of emotions but simply to begin to increase your level of sensitivity to and awareness of your emotional state. Also, becoming aware of the degree to which you are sharing what you are feeling can provide clues, which you will later be able to use to address areas of life in which you want to experience a greater degree of satisfaction.

Just having done this experiment and answering these questions will provide a new level of awareness of your emotional state moving forward. That said, developing a sufficient level of awareness to understand that any emotion that you are experiencing is yours and that no one can force you to feel any particular emotion takes a certain amount of practice over time. And, so, having regular practices in place to get in touch with what you are feeling may be required for you. This is discussed in further detail in Chapter 11.

Range & Depth

While many researchers agree that there are eight basic emotions that all human cultures express (happiness, surprise, anger, fear, disgust, sadness, anticipation and trust), research has also shown that the human face is capable of creating more than 7,000 different facial expressions. So, the third aspect of emotional fluency asks that we explore the full range and depth of our emotional expression.

We have a phenomenal range of emotion available to us so that we can respond appropriately to our environment and the situations we find ourselves in as we move through life. The thing is, for a variety of reasons (cultural, personal, and circumstantial), we begin our training in disconnecting from or numbing some of our emotions at a young age. As time goes on, we continue to dampen or completely avoid certain emotions, until, by the time we've reached adulthood, we have sometimes completely lost some of our emotional capacity.

The impact of this disconnection is profound, though we're often unaware of it. We may find that we're challenged in connection with other people. It can be that we don't develop intimacy easily or that we can only interact well with certain kinds of people. In addition, a reduced range of emotional capacity can limit what activities and situations we allow ourselves to engage with. And so, life can begin to get predictable and boring.

By the time we begin to be aware of the impacts of having disconnected from our full range of emotion, we've generally built up quite a significant number of strategies for avoiding and/or suppressing them. The exercises later in this chapter are designed to help you begin expanding that range again.

In addition to the range, the depth of our emotions is also important to consider. For example, while we may be able to experience brief bouts of happiness regularly, a deeper joy may allude us. Or, we will let ourselves feel annoyed or frustrated but not truly angry.

Ironically, fear, one of our primary emotions, is often the one we are most resistant to feeling and that also keeps us from feeling the other emotions. One of the most common concerns that I've encountered in coaching people about their emotional range and depth is that they are afraid to feel their emotions fully because they think they might "take them over" or they may never be the same if they let themselves go "all the way there." And, in some ways, the fear is called for. Indeed, when we allow ourselves to feel the full power and force of our emotional energy, oftentimes it fuels us to make the changes we must make in our lives. So, it's no wonder the mind thinks this is a bad idea and encourages, with thought projections of what might occur, the emotion of fear.

There is one final note about "going all the way there" with the depth of an emotion. When we finally do let ourselves feel and express the full depth of an emotion, it almost never lasts very long! I have witnessed this so many times in the somatic integration work that I facilitate with people. What typically takes much longer is the resistance to accepting that the emotion is there and/or getting ourselves to the point where we are willing to feel it.

Both In the Moment & After The Fact

Once we've been able to connect with, acknowledge and experience the full depth of a particular emotion with ourselves, the next level of fluency asks us to connect with our emotions while in the presence of another. And so, we come full circle to the example at the beginning of this chapter.

If you'll recall, we used the example of arriving home to find that a request you had made of your partner was not fulfilled upon. Now, here's the thing you want to get about being human. You're not always going to have the presence of mind to express yourself in the best possible way for all involved. And part of this is by design. The true experience of emotion tends to short circuit the mind in just those moments when it would be nice to be able to step back and get some perspective.

And so, the final aspect of emotional fluency is to become more and more skilled at having full conversations, which include emotions during the conversation *and* after the fact. Let's look at these one at a time.

When you initially begin engaging fully with all four aspects of emotional fluency, it's often the case that you'll only be able to see what happened in a particular conversation or situation after the fact. And so, the first skill to develop is to be able to readdress what has happened in the past. This requires both humility and a certain degree of courage to wade back in to a situation or conversation that was not pleasant the first time around. That said, as you learn to be self-referential when discussing your emotions and reactions (see "Owning Our Emotions" above), this becomes easier and easier to do because you are no longer putting the other person on the defensive.

And then, something magic begins to happen. As you begin to gain more and more awareness, both of your emotions and when and how you are conflating your emotions and thoughts, you will have a unique experience. There's no way to know exactly when or how it will occur. Suddenly, in the middle of what seems like the 100th time you are having the same conversation with your boss, lover, or family member, you'll stop. Instead of saying what you normally say, you'll say something like, "You know what I just realized? I'm collapsing my thoughts and emotions right now and I think that's part of why we're not seeing eye to eye here," or "Wait a second! I just realized that the entire time we've been having this conversation, I've been hiding the fact that I'm really scared that you are going to judge me for X, Y, or Z."

This will happen more and more frequently as you continue to bring further awareness to your emotional state and you continue to broaden and deepen your actual experience of your emotions. And the best news about that is that you won't have to return back to conversations from the past as much because you'll be dealing with your emotions as they are happening!

EMOTIONAL AWARENESS EXERCISES

These tools will help you become aware of the semi-conscious emotional cycles and backwaters that we all have, and help you to re-connect with the full range and depth of your emotions. Let's dive in to the different exercises you can engage with to strengthen your connection to this incredibly powerful energy magnifier. You can choose from a wide variety, so your best bet is to read through them all and then choose the one that speaks most directly to you at this time.

"We each have a unique learning style. I recommend that, if after a day or two, you are not expanding your level of awareness, you change the exercise that you are engaging with. Please refer to the Resources&References section, under the header for Chapter 5, to learn more about different learning styles."

Hands Over Heart

This exercise can be done whenever and wherever you can create 60 seconds of privacy and it doesn't get any simpler than that. All you need to do is place your hands on your heart (one on top of the other), press into the skin slightly and ask yourself "What can I allow myself to feel more of right now?" The key to this exercise is to allow the answer to arise from your emotional intelligence and not from your mind. This may take a bit of practice, however, if you keep at it, you will surprise yourself with what shows up.

You can start engaging with this exercise once a day and then up the frequency as you see fit. With this exercise, you are engaging with an intelligence that does not originate in the mind. By beginning with placing the hands on the body and then checking in with the emotions, the mind becomes the observer and focus mechanism without taking over the process.

The only other important aspect is to actually allow yourself to feel the emotion. If you can both acknowledge and then actually experience the emotion, you are well on your way to giving the EM of your emotions a "seat at the table" as you navigate through the process of consciously creating your experience during the day.

The Vessel of Your Emotions

As mentioned in the awareness chapter on body, Somato Respiratory Integration is a tool that I have used to great effect with myself and thousands of others over the years. One of the reasons that SRI is so powerful is that it allows you to choose which EM you want to engage with during the exercises. To that end, there is an audio file available to listen to and practice that will allow you to safely distinguish and experience the particular emotions that you are currently resisting. And then, you'll actually be able to feel what happens when you stop resisting and the effect that this has on the body/mind. I practice these exercises almost every day and reap the energetic rewards! Simply head over to "www.consciousliving.ning.com" to register to join the community for readers of the book and there you'll find a forum which includes the audio file of the SRI exercise.

Turn to Hollywood

The motion picture industry rakes in billions and billions, year in and year out, and with good reason. They have perfected the art and science of coaxing out of all of us a wide range of emotions. Whether it's the latest adult comedy, rom-com, action thriller, or period piece, you will never be short of options for triggering a particular emotional state in you.

For those of you who may find it a bit challenging to connect with your emotions by going directly inward, you may find that this exercise is beneficial for giving you a springboard into your emotional world. To that end, I've gathered together a selection of suggested movie scenes to watch for each of the major emotional states. Some of these you can find quite easily for free on the web. Others you may have in your personal collection. For a list of the suggested scenes, simply turn to the Resources section at the end of the book.

Finally, for some of you, you may find it beneficial to have a pen and paper nearby to write down what these scenes stirred up for you. Try to focus on the emotional reaction and then, separately, on any thoughts associated with your emotions. This will give you practice in generating emotional fluency.

Finding Your Way Back Home

My experience working one-on-one with thousands of people during the past 10 years has shown me that our bodies can actually serve as a very detailed map of our emotional landscape. And we can use that map to direct us back home: back to the experience of peace, calm and connection, which is our birthright and our natural state.

This exercise is particularly useful when you find yourself in an emotional state other than calm and peaceful. To begin, get present to the primary emotion that you are aware of in the present moment. For some people, it's helpful to close the eyes. Once you get present to the emotion, see if you can notice where in the body "resonates with" or corresponds to that emotion.

Once you've located that place, let yourself feel the emotion for a minimum of 10 seconds. If the emotion is anger, you may want to squeeze the hands into fists. If it's sadness, you may want to let your shoulders slump. In all cases, allow your face to express the emotion fully.

Next, take three long breaths in the nose and out the mouth to re-center yourself. Often, at this point in the exercise, you may already be feeling a greater degree of calm and peace. If that's the case, all there is left to do is notice where in your body most resonates with that sense of peace and calm. You can bring your hands there and simply enjoy that sensation as long as you'd like.

If you aren't yet feeling peace and calm, you can repeat the exercise once or twice more. Sometimes, you may find that there is another emotion buried underneath the first one. If that's the case, repeat the exercise for that emotion.

If after the third time you still don't find peace and calm, not to worry. You have two additional options. You can recall a moment in time or situation in the past in which you were totally calm and at peace. Or, if even that is a challenge in this particular moment, you can imagine a situation that you feel would bring you peace and calm such as, curled up in a hammock over-looking a turquoise sea with palm trees rustling in the wind.

Just one final note on this exercise. There are times when the emotion you are connecting with is quite intense. If this is the case, I have two recommendations. One is that you set aside a sufficient amount of time (up to five minutes) to feel the full extent of the emotion. And two is that you be vigilant for thoughts entering into the mix! One of the surest ways to prolong an unpleasant emotion is to allow the mind to feed that emotion with thoughts that only serve to lengthen the amount of time you are feeling the unpleasantness while not allowing you to *fully feel* the unfiltered, raw emotion.

Distinguishing Thoughts From Emotions

As we discussed earlier in this chapter, the first core competency for emotional fluency is the capacity to distinguish the difference between our thoughts and our emotions. This exercise is designed to build this muscle by giving you the opportunity to identify instances of thought/emotion collapse during the day, as they're happening, and then re-address them when you have the time and space to do so. These instances will show up for you as an interruption in the flow of your day when you notice that you experiencing fear, anger, or sadness for longer than five to 10 minutes.

You'll want to have a designated way to capture what you'll be writing down when you encounter a situation in your day-to-day life. If you have a smart phone, this is ideal as it is most likely always with you. And, you then have the option of recording an audio rather than typing. If not, you'll need to get in the habit of carrying around a piece of paper and pen with you at all times. The power of this exercise comes in being able to swiftly and accurately capture both your thoughts and your emotional state during or just after you notice the interruption in the flow of your day.

Once you've got these logistics sorted out, capture three things each time there's an interruption in the flow. First, rate the intensity of the interruption on a scale from 1 to 10, 1. being barely noticeable, 10. being nearly paralyzed. Then, simply write a few sentences that accurately reflect the thoughts running through your mind related to this interruption in flow. Finally, identify the primary emotion from amongst the following: fear, sadness, anger, disgust.

Then, choose a time during your day (perhaps in the evening after dinner or before sleep) when you can review the instances from the day. Sometimes, all that's needed is for you to reflect and get the relationship between the thoughts and the emotion and you'll have the insight you need. Other times, you may see that there is a conversation to have or some new way to approach the situation that triggered the interruption in flow. If that's the case, write this down and highlight it in some way (circle it or bold the words if you're using a digital device) so that when you return the next day you will be reminded to check and see whether you had the conversation or took some new action.

Emotions Without Explanation

Now this one can be a lot of fun.☺ The idea is to practice expressing your emotional state with no explanation. This can take many forms. You can simply begin sharing your emotional state with those closest to you and/or asking them what their emotional state is. One easy way to begin is to ask "How are you feeling?" rather than "How are you?"

Initially, it can feel a bit strange to share yourself in this way. You may find that there is a strong desire to explain your emotional state, especially if it's an emotion that either you or the person you are sharing it with has a hard time being present with. This desire is just the habit that most of us have, to some degree, of automatically attaching thoughts and analysis to our emotional state. You may find that you need to explain a bit about the exercise you are practicing.

As you begin to get more practiced with this way of communicating and the people around you begin to get used to this kind of expression, you can extend it to email, texts, and the like. And then, begin to notice the shift in the quality of your connection to other people. See if you experience a greater sense of intensity or intimacy with the people around you whom you care the most about.

Oh, and remember, you are practicing sharing your emotions and nothing else. This is not about blaming anyone else. It's about increasing your capacity to express the full range and depth of your emotional landscape.

Wading into the ocean of emotions can be a bit like a first dip in the sea or lake in the late spring or early summer. It can be a bit uncomfortable or shocking at times, but you know that you always feel more alive afterward and are glad that you did it!

I also know that emotions can sometimes be very intense and unpleasant. Take your time and ease into this exploration. If you find a particular exercise is a bit much for you, choose another one. And, finally, turn to those people in your life that love you for support. Share with them your journey so that you can have the experience that all is well as you navigate the sometimes-stormy emotional seas.

Remember, these exercises are my best suggestions for dealing directly with the energetic magnifiers. You are welcome to leverage exercises or modalities that you are already familiar with, search out new ones, or create your own! For the most up-to-date thinking on all of these exercises and to share your experience or get support, you can head over to www.consciousliving.ning.com to register for access to the online community.

CHAPTER 7

IT'S A MIN(D)FIELD

I was living so many people's dream life in Barcelona and then found myself in the midst of a separation from my partner of nearly eight years. My friend Otto comes in to town for a visit and we're strolling along one of the many pedestrian *calles* in Barcelona. There are no cars, just lots of outside seating and lively conversation. It's early October, but still warm enough to be walking outside in the evening in shorts and no jacket. I begin telling him some of the details of the story of how the separation occurred and he literally stops me in my tracks by grabbing my arm before I can even get going.

He says to me, "Are you hearing yourself?" I say "Of course." He says, "No, can you not hear that you are taking no responsibility for how your life is in this moment? Snap out of it!"

We went on to have a long conversation which then spawned a series of conversations with people in my life that returned me to power in my thinking and my approach to my life. Over the next week, Otto and I took a surgeon's knife to my thinking and I got into Committed Action mode for the Mind and began to shift my reality.

One never stops expanding in their mental awareness during this lifetime.

When you stop and consider it, the sheer stamina of the mind is absolutely astonishing. Every second of your waking life, your mind is churning out thought after thought after thought, with no end in sight. It doesn't stop when you are listening to someone else speak or when you're speaking. It doesn't even stop when you're having sex or when you're eating. There is even a wealth of scientific evidence for how active the mind is while you're sleeping. In many ways, we are slaves to our minds and the never-ending river of thoughts that flow through them.

We know that there is plenty of thinking going on in the animal kingdom as well. The particular challenge for us human beings is that not every thought that comes through our minds is a constructive one. We are the only living beings that we're aware of that have thoughts that disempower us and restrict our behavior. There are particular loops of thought that we can get caught in that waste time and energy. Very often, our thoughts are not at all about our current experience. Much of the time we are either re-living a past event or thinking about and/or worrying about a possible future occurrence. And so, most of the time, we're not all connected to what is actually happening around us.

I can still remember the moment that I experienced, for the first time, the power that's available to me when my thoughts are not focused on the past or future but based completely in the present moment. I was sitting in a basement near Madison Square Garden with 150 or so other people. We had been there for two and a half days attending a course given by Landmark Education called the Landmark Forum. We had just been led through a unique exercise that involved getting present to the visceral bodily sensations and emotions associated with the level of fear of other people that all human beings are almost constantly feeling, but pushing down. And then, at a particular moment toward the very end of the exercise, something bloomed in my mind. I experienced a clarity and a presence that I can only describe as spacious and slightly amusing. In that moment, I understood that, while I will never be able to quiet my mind or stop it from thinking, I have a choice in every moment to associate or not with those thoughts. And I also had the knowing that if I could choose what thoughts I focused on, anything truly was possible.

In order to have the exploration of the Energy Magnifier of the mind be a process that is as easeful as possible for you, there are four critical distinctions for you to understand. Let's walk through them one by one.

Consider That Your Thoughts Are Almost Always Borrowed

Part of the reason why we find it so challenging, at times, to gain perspective on our thinking is that we think that all the thoughts that we're thinking are ours. We are then so attached to them that they become rigid and "true," limiting us from considering other ones. But when you really stop and consider it, how many of the thoughts that you have in a given day are completely new, as in, have never been thought before by another human being? Of course, it happens sometimes! But it's actually quite rare. Most of the thoughts we're thinking, we have actually borrowed from someone else.

Many of the thoughts and thought patterns that we are giving our attention to day to day originate with our families. As we grow up, we learn what kind of thinking and what particular thoughts are acceptable. We learn which ones lead to greater acceptance for us and which ones people around us are not as comfortable with. Of course, to varying degrees, we develop our personality to be one that either mostly conforms to the group or mostly individuates. That said, even when we individuate, we are doing so *in response* to the existing thoughts and thought structures. Typically, we then look outside the family structure for other communities and groups of people that have different thinking. Again, we borrow existing thoughts rather than coming up with our own. And, it makes sense. It takes a lot of energy to come up with original thought!

This process continues over and over and over again. Maybe you go to college and get exposed to a much larger world of thought. Even then, you're choosing from an existing buffet table of thoughts. And on, and on, and on.

I want to be clear that there are exceptions to this rule. Clearly, original thought occurs. And, my intention in highlighting this aspect of reality is to bring you freedom, joy and power, not to have you feeling insufficient or dim. Consider it good news to know that your thoughts are not your own. Here's why: you can actually choose other thoughts if the ones you're currently attached to are not serving you. Most of the exercises later in this chapter are aimed at both increasing your awareness of your current thinking and encouraging your experience of the elasticity of thinking. As you increase your flexibility of thinking, you will find that you are able to maintain an empowered state, even as the world and people around you continue to change at varying and sometimes dizzying speeds.

Thoughts vs. Perspectives

The next thing to get about the thinking mind is that there are individual thoughts and then there are larger narratives about the world. These larger narratives, or perspectives, play an important role in determining which individual thoughts you will come up with in response to a particular conversation or situation. It points to the reason why we often try and fail to change our thinking. We focus on individual thoughts rather than the perspective that is keeping those thoughts in place.

Let's consider a practical example. You're sitting on an airplane flying from New York to Mexico City. You happen to be seated next to a mother and her young child. As the flight begins you notice that the child is regularly brushing up against you and attempting to engage you in conversation and in whatever game or activity they are busy with. Your initial thought goes something like, "This child is quite precocious." As the flight enters its third hour with no sign of the mother responding to your plaintive looks for help, you then have the thought, "This woman is not a very considerate person or good mother." By the end of the flight, your thoughts are no longer appropriate for this family book. ;)

The thing is, for each of these thoughts (and all the other ones in between) there is an over-arching perspective from which they hang, like the structure from which the individual elements of a baby's mobile hang from. In this instance, it could be something like, "Being aware of other people's personal space is a sign of respect." You can see that all the individual thoughts you were having about this child make sense if this is the worldview that you have. Remember, almost all of the worldviews you have are "borrowed" from your family, peer groups, or historical lines of thought.

The real power with this distinction comes when we also consider what the perspective of the child's mother is. It could be something like, "Being relaxed and comfortable in the presence of others is a sign of respect." If you can imagine what another's over-arching perspective might be in any given situation, what they are thinking, saying, doing, or not doing will make a whole lot more sense.

When we evaluate our thinking from this understanding, there is often significant insight into what's actually going on rather than a fixation on the individual thoughts you are thinking. I've found that the majority of mental stress that I encounter has its roots in my attachment, not just to individual thoughts but to some worldview or perspective on how things are or how they're "supposed to be."

In fact, understanding this concept is fundamental to being able to effectively and lovingly connect with people that are not already in the same worldview or perspective as you. When you master this distinction, you will find that you capacity to connect with a wide range of different people is significantly enhanced.

Empowered vs. Disempowered

Left to its own devices, our mind is not particularly choosy when it comes to which thoughts it's churning out. So if we are not paying attention, we may be at the mercy of thoughts that are leaving us in a disempowered state. And what distinguishes a disempowered thought from an empowered one? Well, there are certain key indicators for disempowerment which are easily recognized.

The first is that your emotional state is stuck or stagnant. If you notice that you have been feeling a particular emotion for more than 10 minutes, the chances are that your thinking is disempowered. In other words, the thoughts you are having and/ or the perspective you are holding are leading to an unwanted emotional experience. Being able to distinguish when this is happening and having tools to "flip the script" in your mind is an incredibly powerful and useful tool for living a consciously empowered life.

Imagine you are just finishing up a fantastic dinner with a group of friends in New York City. It's time to pay the bill and as everyone is placing their money for their portion of the bill on the table, you notice that your friend Lindsay is only adding in 5% for the tip. Now, tipping is different in different countries, however you know that the average tip is 15 to 20 percent in the U.S. As things wind down at the restaurant and everyone is heading for the door, you notice that your emotional state is predominantly one of frustration. As the group heads to a nearby bar for a drink, you notice that you are still frustrated and can't quite seem to shake it.

Most people, in this situation, will simply do nothing about the emotion. Instead, they will begin (or continue) putting together a narrative for how stingy this one friend is. You are now more or less setting yourself up for more frustration each and every time you are around this friend of yours and money is involved. By not dealing with the emotion in the moment, you are doomed to have to experience it again later (either with this friend or with someone else).

If, instead, you took a moment to distinguish your thoughts and your over-arching perspective, you'd have an opportunity to shift your emotional state and fully enjoy the rest of your evening. In this case, perhaps the thought is "Lindsay is cheap" or "Lindsay cares only about herself and not about how it will look if we leave less than a 15 percent tip as a group." Sometimes, just getting crystal clear about the actual thoughts that are leading to your emotional state is enough to shift it.

But, you can take it a step further. You can ask yourself what perspective is leading to the thought "Lindsay is cheap." You might see that the over-arching viewpoint you hold when it comes to the situation as a whole is, "People who work for tips should always be given a 15 percent tip, unless they are rude or dismissive in their service." Once you can see the perspective that's giving you the thoughts, which are giving you the emotional state, you have the keys to unlocking the emotions and letting them flow again. And then, you can decide whether you want to share the whole thing with your friend with an aim toward creating a space for increased understanding between the two of you.

In the above example, the stuck emotion is actually an opportunity in disguise. Almost always, when strong emotions are present, they are pointing us to the awareness that we actually care about the other person or about how they or you are being perceived by others in the situation. And so, you have the chance to now take the relationship with this person to a deeper level where you are able to talk about reactions you might be having, emotions you might be feeling and reveal to them more about yourself, including your perspectives on how the world is or how things should be. Of course, with every opportunity, comes a risk! The person may not be up for that level of relationship with you. And there is one other danger. If you remain attached to your perspective as the only correct one, there will be no chance for connection with the other person.

All of this may seem very overwhelming initially. I know it was for me! But, what's the alternative? Well, the alternative is that you are stuck with repeating emotional patterns and a kind of stagnation in your relationships and life experiences. Sure, it's safer, but it's just not going to lead to the kind of deep satisfaction that's available when you know, beyond the shadow of a doubt, that you are able to empower yourself no matter what emotion you are experiencing or what situation you are facing.

Another very clear indicator that your thinking is disempowered will show up in the conversations around you. If you notice that the conversation you are having is similar to a conversation you've had in the past *and* that it's resulting in recurring unpleasant emotional responses for you, it's quite likely that your thinking is not empowered. Most of the time, in these instances, it's smart to first distinguish your emotions from your thoughts (see Chapter 6 for more on this). You can then begin looking at what perspective is "running the show" and re-approach the conversation with that person, letting them know what you have seen.

Maybe you've had a situation similar to this one. Let's say your having a video conversation with your Mom. The conversation is pleasant and cordial for a while and then comes the inevitable question, "So, are you dating anyone?" It's probably the 100th time she's asked you this question, but your emotional response is the same every time. You're annoyed and it impacts the rest of the conversation because you have now closed down in some way.

What's great about recurring conversations is that, if you are having one with someone, it means that you are in some kind of longer term relationship with them. So, there is a much higher chance that this person cares about you enough to explore new ways of communicating and relating. In this way, the risk is lower but in another way it's higher. Why? Because it's likely that the person you are having a recurring conversation with is very important to you on some level since you've been "putting up" with the recurring conversation for so long. ☺ And so, the stakes are a bit higher.

In this example, the thoughts that are associated with the emotion could be something like, "Why can't she just let me be for once?" or "How come she doesn't ask me whether I'm happy instead of asking me if I'm dating someone?" Now, just in distinguishing those thoughts, you have the beginning of a new way of operating in this conversation with your Mom. Often, the pathway out of the dense forest of this recurring conversation is already there. It's in the questions that you are thinking but not asking. And, so, one way forward is simply to ask, with genuine curiosity, "Mom, why do you almost always ask me if I'm dating someone?" By posing this question, at least you are honoring the emotional response you are having and you have a chance to actually get to know a little bit more about what's driving the recurring dialogue.

But, let's take it a step further. If you were to look at your worldview or perspective about this situation it might be something like, "Mothers should be concerned with their children's happiness above all else." And if you were to see this as your worldview you could then have a conversation with your Mom where you share that with her and/or ask her why it is that she asks that question. By asking her that question, you would be able to get close to her worldview and understand where she is coming from when she has the thought to ask you the question about whether you're dating anyone.

When you have done the work to see how the emotions are given by the thoughts and how the thoughts are given by the perspective you have, you will come to any conversation with a different tone. And, you will find that there is more space for real connection and communication rather than two perspectives broadcasting to each other with no one receiving.

This leads us to the fourth and final critical distinction to have in the background as you step consciously into the forest of the mind.

Simultaneous Broadcasting vs. True Communication

As we discussed at the beginning of the chapter, the mind is always thinking. Whether or not you are doing something, talking to someone else or just sitting down in a café having a warm beverage, there is a conversation going on. And it's a one-way conversation, between you and you, which impacts you moment to moment. You're basically listening to whatever you are thinking, all the time.

This reality makes it very challenging to actually hear what other people are saying to you. I don't mean with your ears, I mean actually register what they are saying without regularly shifting your attention back to what you mind is already throwing at you. Your mind is saying things to you about how this person looks, is judging and assessing the validity of what they are saying, and is also coming up with something to respond with when the other person stops talking. As a result, there is actually very little space for listening to what the person is *actually saying*.

When there are two people in a conversation, and both of them are at the mercy of their internal monologue, we end up with two broadcasters and no receivers. Many relationships get stagnant thanks to this kind of communication. It's also why there is so much opportunity for misunderstanding, conflict, and the experience of not feeling connected to those we care about.

So, how do we deal with this? As discussed, we know we can't stop the mind from generating thoughts. Instead, we leverage the mind by engaging it directly with what the other person is saying. One way is simply to pause, briefly, after someone has finished talking to review in your mind what they just said. In this way, you can be sure you are responding to what they said rather than to your internal dialogue.

Another way to harness the mind to actually hear what someone is saying is to repeat back to the person what you heard them say (or a portion of what you heard them say) before you respond. In this way, you assure the other person that you are listening and also have a clearer sense of what's been said so that you have a better chance of having a constructive and connective conversation.

MENTAL EXERCISES

With the following exercises, you'll be exploring the landscape of your thinking and have the opportunity to experience a new level of awareness and clarity about, your thoughts and thought patterns. There is a wide variety to choose from, so your best bet is to read through them all and then choose the one that speaks most directly to you at this time. We will take many of these exercises further when it's time for Committed Action mode. Here in Awareness Mode, the focus is on expanding and deepening awareness first.

Exposing The Monologue

The intention with this exercise is simply to bring a higher degree of awareness to the *quality* of your thinking and to begin to develop your capacity to influence your thinking over time.

You begin by increasing your level of awareness. Take 2 to 3 minutes either prior to sleeping or soon after waking to write down your thoughts. You are simply writing down what you are thinking. In the beginning, much of your thinking may actually refer to the very exercise that you're engaged with as your brain gets used to the fact that you are doing it. You may also find that you are resistant to writing down your thoughts. Usually this is because your mind knows, on some level, that it's days are numbered if you were to actually focus on some of the useless and/or disempowering thoughts that it's throwing at you. ☺ With repetition, you will relax into a rhythm and get quite comfortable.

There is more to this exercise in Committed Action mode. Here in Awareness Mode, it's about expanding your awareness first. So, resist the urge to do something about the thoughts and simply allow the time to fully get the pervasiveness of your thinking.

This exercise is a simple, but very direct, way of beginning to interact with your thoughts in a way that is something other than passive. While it takes time to master the art of interacting with them in a way that leaves you fully empowered, the simple act of exposing thoughts to your conscious awareness begins to shift what's possible for you in your life.

Your Customized Personal Mantra

Because your mind can really only focus on one thought in any given moment, this exercise can be a very powerful way to string together two thoughts in a way that empowers you. The first step is to acknowledge a disempowering thought you've had in the last couple of days. It could be something like, "I don't know if I'm on the right track in my life" or "I was such an idiot last night at dinner with my partner." Write this down. Next, you'll identify an empowered thought that makes sense to you in the following construct, "Even though I have the thought that I was such an idiot last night at dinner with my partner, I know that...." So, in this example, it might be "I know that I'm worthy of love even when I act like an idiot." Write this down as well.

There are two pieces to this exercise that are critical to its success. The first is that the empowered thought must ring true for you. It must be something you believe to be true and that helps you to step back from the disempowered thought. The idea is **not** to ignore or change the disempowered thought. Instead, the intention is that you are able to take a wider/different view on it by affirming your empowerment *even though* you sometimes have disempowered thoughts.

The second critical piece is that when you are reading/saying the phrase to yourself, that you are focused on actually thinking it rather than simply reading/saying it. Now, from time to time, you will go into a bit of a trance and just be reading/saying it. That's fine. Simply return yourself to actually *generating* the thought rather than just repeating it.

Scheduling Empowerment Via Mining Your Thoughts

Believe it or not, some of us operate in a significantly more empowered state when we spend time organizing and scheduling our day, week, and month toward the aim of maximizing our experience of satisfied living. If this sounds like you, then this is a great exercise to engage with.

You'll start by pulling up or getting out your calendar. Next, as you consider the past 24 hours, see if you can identify the time when you were in the most disempowered mental state. Of course, some days will feature more intense bouts of disempowerment than others.

Once you have identified the time frame, see if you can notice anything significant about it. For example, was the disempowered thinking a one-off occurrence or something that is cyclical and repeating? Did the situation involve a particular person around whom you tend to be disempowered in your thinking? Was there a particular activity you were engaged with that has resulted in your being disempowered in your thinking more than once in the past?

What you are looking for is some thread that you can pull upon to shake loose the pattern of disempowered thinking. When you do this, you are then able to begin coming up with alternate ways to structure your day, week, or month. For example, if you notice that you are often disempowered in your thinking when you are leaving the morning staff meeting, you may see that a quick check in with one of your co-workers before the meeting is what's needed. Or, perhaps you have an idea for a new way to structure the meeting that could yield more effective results for the team.

Of course, your disempowered thinking may be related to a family member or even your health and well-being. In any event, your job is to identify one new action you can take that has a chance of busting up the existing string of events that results in your disempowered thinking. And then, take that action. It may not yield the result you are hoping for right away, but you are guaranteed to learn more of what you need to see in order to be able to ultimately shift what's happening. And, you may strike gold on the first try!

Voices Outside Your Head

This is a really fun and perhaps somewhat edgy (culturally) exercise that can very quickly move you from disempowered to just plain laughing at yourself. ☺

When you find yourself stuck in a disempowered mental state, whip out your smartphone, plug in the earbuds, and hit the record button. Then, just start speaking out loud what you are thinking. The good news is that there are so many people these days that are talking into their smartphones (either on phone conversations or into speech-to-text software) that you're far less likely to get the kind of stares you may have gotten five or ten years ago. ☺

Initially, you will likely notice that you are resistant to saying out loud what you're thinking. Even more than the earlier exercise, which involved writing down your thoughts, speaking them aloud can be particularly confronting for you. However, this is exactly why this exercise is so powerful. As you begin to drag your disempowered thinking from the foggy corners of your mind out into the world through your spoken words, you will very likely be somewhat amused at what it is that you are saying to yourself. I have encountered this phenomenon countless times with my coaching clients and have witnessed the incredible shifts that people experience when they are able to reflect on what it is that they are saying to themselves in their minds.

The key to this exercise is to ensure that you then put aside the recording for the rest of the day and then listen to it only one time in the next 24 hours. I recommend you don't do this shortly before sleeping or shortly after waking, as we don't want to disturb your ability to fall asleep or start your day off on the wrong foot with a gusher of disempowered thinking. Instead, look for a time when you are particularly empowered in your thinking, like after a nice workout or an uplifting conversation with a friend or colleague. Then, plug those headphones in again and listen to what you were thinking to yourself earlier. If you notice particular phrases or thoughts that you can now see differently, write those down. Being able to see the malleability and changeability of our thinking is a critical tool in decreasing the amount of time we spend being disempowered as we train ourselves to look for the next opportunity for empowered thinking.

Distinguishing Thoughts From Emotions

You will find this exercise in both the awareness chapter for emotions and mind. It's designed to build your capacity to identify instances of thought/emotion collapse during the day, as they're happening, and then re-address them when you have the time and space to do so. These instances will show up for you as an interruption in the flow of your day when you notice that you are stuck in some kind of repeating thought pattern for longer than five to 10 minutes.

You'll want to have a designated way to capture what you'll be writing down when you encounter a situation in your day-to-day life. If you have a smart phone, this is ideal as it is most likely always with you. And, you then have the option of recording an audio rather than typing. If not, you'll need to get in the habit of carrying around a piece of paper and pen with you at all times. The power of this exercise comes in being able to swiftly and accurately capture both your thoughts and your emotional state during or just after you notice the interruption in the flow of your day.

Once you've got these logistics sorted out, capture three things each time there's an interruption in the flow. First, rate the intensity of the interruption on a scale from 1 to 10, 1. being barely noticeable, 10. being nearly paralyzed. Then, simply write a few sentences that accurately reflect the thoughts running through your mind related to this interruption in flow. Finally, identify the primary emotion from among the following (fear, sadness, anger, disgust).

Then, choose a time during your day (perhaps in the evening after dinner or before sleep) when you can review the instances from the day. Sometimes, all that's needed is for you to reflect and get the relationship between the thoughts and the primary emotion and you'll have the insight you need. Other times, you may see that there is a conversation to have or some new way to approach the situation that triggered the interruption in flow. If that's the case, write this down and highlight it in some way (circle it or bold the words if you're using a digital device) so that when you return the next day, you will be reminded to check and see whether you had the conversation or took some new action.

Change Your Position

I employ this exercise almost every single day when I notice my mental energy beginning to ebb. It's deceptively simple yet highly effective for many people. It involves shifting either the physical space you are in or the way your body is positioned. For this exercise to be effective, you don't need to be in a particularly disempowered mental state.

There are two engagement levels for this exercise. First, if you are a bit short on time, you'll simply be changing the way your body is positioned. For most of us, there are three main positions that our bodies are in during a given day. These are: lying down, sitting, or standing up. When you are looking for a boost in your clarity of thinking, shifting from your current position to another one for as little as two to three minutes can have an impressive impact. And, I must say, if it's safe to do so and the people around you can handle it, a handstand against a wall (or even just legs up the wall) is my favorite! But, it's perfectly fine to just go find a room that's not in use where you are and lay down for a few minutes. Or, if even just taking a walk to fill up your bottle or glass of water can work.

The reality is, you are likely already doing some version of this, naturally. The key here is to increase you level of sensitivity to, and decrease your level of tolerance for, unclear or disempowered thinking.

The second level of engagement involves actually changing up the space you are in. This works best if you have a bit more time. So, if you've been in a particular room or desk space for longer than 30 minutes or so, shift it up and set yourself up somewhere else in your house or at your office. If you've been inside for longer than a couple of hours, go outside (yes, even if it's too cold or too hot!). Or, if you've got the flexibility, take your computer and head to a coffee shop or go sit outside at a park for a while.

I don't know exactly how much of the impact of this exercise comes down to the shift in blood flow to the brain and how much has to do with changing up your peripheral scenery. All I know, from personal experience, is that it's the simplest and most reliable way to boost my mental clarity, and for that reason, I use it every day.

The Body-Mind Connection

As mentioned in the awareness chapters on body and emotion, Somato Respiratory Integration is a tool that I have used to great affect, with both myself and thousands of others, over the years. One of the reasons that SRI is so powerful is that it allows you to choose which EM you want to engage with during the exercises. To that end, there is an audio file available to listen to and practice that will allow you to safely distinguish and experience the particular thoughts that are disempowering you. And then, you'll actually be able to feel what happens when you stop resisting having those thoughts and the effect that this has on the body/mind. I practice these exercises almost every day and reap the energetic rewards! Simply head over to "www.consciousliving.ning.com to register to join the community for readers of the book and there you'll find a forum which includes the audio file of the SRI exercise.

What I've learned in my 10+ years of near constant self development and coaching is this: while it's not likely that I'll ever find the off switch for my ever-thinking mind, any one of the exercises outlined above can provide me with a new level of awareness. Even though we can't turn off the supercomputer that is our brain, we can install new software and these exercises are the different software packages. Install one or two of them and be sure to share how it's going with the larger community at www. consciousliving.ning.com.

Remember, these exercises are my best suggestions for dealing directly with the energy magnifiers. You are welcome to leverage exercises or modalities that you are already familiar with, search out new ones or create your own!

CHAPTER 8

THE YOU BEYOND YOUR MIND

If you've found yourself at the beginning of this chapter, I'm assuming you got here in one of two ways. One way is that you are beginning your One Week Life Satisfaction Booster (see Chapter 4) and already have a clear understanding that there is something available for you if you tap into the Energy Magnifier that is the capital "s" Self. You can sense that truly conscious, satisfied living is currently beyond your reach and no amount of tending to and connecting to your body, emotions and mind is going to help you to reach it.

The second way you may be beginning this chapter is after just having read the awareness chapters on body, emotion and mind. If this is the case, you may not be wholly open to the idea of actively engaging with what has been called everything from "higher self" to soul to spirit. My job, by the end of this chapter, is to have you clear about the practical benefits which come from connecting to this limitless energy magnifier.

In fact, I would assert that this chapter and its exercises are especially useful for those who have negative concepts about spirit, soul or anything "New Agey." That being said, if you are set on disproving or resisting an experience beyond your rational mind, you will be proven right and will forfeit the opportunity to fully engage with this Energy Magnifier.

I'd like to share with you a bit about my first direct experience of myself as something other than a bag of bones in a sea of emotion with a never quiet mind. It was in the spring of 2001 and the company I worked for hosted a health fair with all manner of practitioners offering modalities I had never heard of before. I tried reflexology and even had my body fat percentage somehow checked by squeezing some kind of device with my hand. At the very end of the day, something made me pop my head into the room where the Reiki practitioner was situated. She was actually already working with someone and I had no idea what she was doing. She was slowly moving her hands around approximately a foot away from my co-worker's body while he had his eyes closed. We locked eyes and she nodded to indicate that I could come over. She pulled a chair up next to my co-worker and invited me to sit down. What happened in the next few minutes would change the course of the rest of my life.

I actually don't know how long I was sitting there before what happened, happened. All I remember is that if felt like something shot out of the side of my neck. The best way I can describe it is like some kind of flash of light, which had emanated from within me, was no longer in me. That one occurrence, which was totally unexpected and certainly not something I was even looking for, shifted everything. I not only understood but actually experienced that there are aspects of the physical world that I can't necessarily see with my eyes or fully understand with my mind. But they do, in reality, exist.

Now, I can't say whether you will have an experience like this in your lifetime. What I can say is that, whether you like it or not, you have connected to the EM of the Self before. It can happen in an instant. Maybe you're present during or just after the birth of a baby. Maybe you've either been the athlete or watched the athlete that performed something so skillful that it transcended the particular sport you/he/she was playing. Instead, it was beauty, or art, or grace in action. You may have had your breath taken away by some natural scene or some encounter with an animal in its wild habitat.

Every one of these moments puts you directly, immediately, and urgently into a state of awe. It's as if your mind can't grasp what is happening with the limited language of thought. When we're in this state of awe, nothing else actually matters. In that moment, we tap into a profound presence as the past and future fall away. All that matters is being in the presence of whatever it was that finally short-circuited your mind for these precious moments.

The vast majority of human beings live their entire life on the planet with a vague but persistent sense that there is something more to life than what they are perceiving through their bodily senses, emotions, and thoughts. But they don't know what this "something" is or how to tap into it.

This chapter is designed to assist you to understand this aspect of yourself and how to actively create the conditions that allow for a more frequent connection to it.

That said, it's important to delineate the intersection, or lack thereof, between the world of religion and the energy magnifier of Self that we are discussing in this chapter.

Almost all of the major wisdom traditions/religions discuss the existence of a world beyond the physical planet Earth that we're living on. For those who adhere to these religions, that one takes a non-physical form after one dies is accepted as reality even though they have no direct evidence. And so, the concept that part of you is not your body, emotions, or thoughts is not too far of a stretch for many.

There are also people in certain wisdom traditions (for example, Buddhism) and others, such as atheists or agnostics, who don't subscribe to the idea that we exist as a *distinct* soul beyond this lifetime. The good news is that whether or not you are a Christian, Jew, Muslim, Buddhist, or atheist, the energy magnifier of the Self is something that you can connect with now, during this lifetime. As we've discussed, you already have been.

Before we dive into the different gateways or access points that exist for experiencing the EM of Self, let's look at bit more closely at why it is that we would want to.

The best reason that I can think of to connect with the Energy Magnifier of Self is that, more times than not, it actually feels really good. ☺ Now, don't get me wrong. True connection to the divine is often something that requires a fair bit of struggle and dedication (mostly because of how strongly we take comfort in our mind as a safety blanket). But, in my experience, the challenge has always been far outweighed by the reward.

Part of why it feels so good to connect to Self is that, for those brief moments, you are no longer protecting yourself, resisting anything that's happening in your life, or either reviewing a past event or planning for a future one. Instead, all of the energy that your brain, nervous system, and body are typically consuming in the process of not being in the present moment, is suddenly available to you right now. This, to me, explains the rush that connecting to Self offers us.

The second reason why it makes sense to connect with Self is that it has the very real potential to beneficially impact the other three EMs. For example, meditation is a great way to connect to our Self. Hundreds of studies on meditation have shown it to generate a variety of benefits: everything from a reduced need for sleep to an elevation of positive emotions to an increase in our mental perceptual capacities. Let's take a closer look at the benefits for each of the EMs related to just this one method of connecting to Self.

Body

Research done by Yale, Harvard and MIT has shown that the actual cortical thickness of people's brains increases, for those practicing meditation, in the areas of the brain that deal with sensory, auditory and visual perception. While the study did not delve into the how or the why behind these changes, what this study shows is that there is a noticeable correlation between meditation and brain physiology. In addition, the research showed that regular meditation may actually slow age-related thinning of the frontal cortex. You can turn to the References section at the end of the book to be pointed to the raw research.

Now, what might this mean in practical terms? Well, if you consider that an increase in awareness of sensory stimuli allows you to more acutely assess a given situation, your capacity to pick up on subtle auditory, visual and other sensory cues would expand. This, in turn, improves the quality of your connection with others and hence your relationships.

Emotions

The author and University of Wisconsin professor Richard Davidson, along with the renowned meditation teacher and medical researcher Jon Kabat-Zinn, have studied the impact of meditation on the brain. The results from Davidson and Kabat-Zinn's research have shown that the left prefrontal cortex, which is the part of the brain associated with, among other things personality expression, demonstrates an increased level of activity among those who meditate. This area of the brain is also specifically associated with happiness.

In day-to-day life, when you're happy, the activity level in your left prefrontal cortex goes up. What studies have shown is that meditation can positively impact the activity level in this area of your brain, leading to increased levels of happiness throughout your day. Other studies have shown meditation's impact on reducing episodes of depression, increasing self-esteem, and reduced anxiety.

Mind

One of the most useful functions of the human mind is its capacity to provide us with creative solutions to life's challenges. Here too, meditation has an impact. According to a 2011 study conducted in the Netherlands, those who meditated in a specific way known as Open Monitoring (which is a distinct form of meditation that aims to increase your capacity to maintain a single point of focus) showed a measurable increase in their creative capacity. Specifically, they were able to come up with a longer list of potential uses for a particular object (brick, shoe, newspaper, etc.), which is a measure for "divergent thinking", a style of thinking that generates multiple ideas or approaches to a single problem.

From a practical point of view, to be able to consistently and successfully come up with multiple solutions to life's challenges or consider multiple possible futures is a skill that is certainly worth developing. This capacity to think "outside the box" is increasingly valuable as we are now living lives that are less beholden to past cultural norms and more in line with our own design, led by our dreams and desires.

The third and final reason for connecting to Self is right there in the word. So much of daily living is now consumed by a deluge of external stimulation and information that we are less and less likely to ever be truly with ourselves and only ourselves. In the 21st century, we have expanded our daily social life beyond just family and friends to now include vast (though looser) global social networks. These networks never stop flowing with pictures, videos, articles, and life updates from all around the world. And because we are social creatures that are wired to seek belonging and stay up to date on what's going on in our social circle, we are spending more and more time browsing through status updates of people we may possibly never see again in our lifetimes.

Then there is the massive expansion of advertising messages. A market research firm concluded that the average city dweller is now receiving up to 5,000 (yes, that's three zeroes) advertising messages per day. This is up from 2,000 in the late 1970's. In addition, the amount of time we are spending with a screen of some kind has risen dramatically each decade. This constant barrage of moving imagery, while stimulating and exciting is also quite confusing and stressful for our sympathetic nervous system which is responsible for maintaining vigilance for any action we may need to take to protect ourselves.

When you combine the physical stress on the sympathetic nervous system from the increase in time spent watching videos *with* the emotional roller coaster that our expanded social networks have us on *with* the mental demands that are a result of the advertising, texts, emails, etc. we are bombarded with, we have the perfect storm for pulling us further and further away from our Selves.

The good news is that there are many ways to find our way back to home base. That's right, meditation, while highly effective, is not the only way to get there! Before we get into the descriptions for specific exercises that you can engage with, let's take a look at the broad categories that offer us access to the EM of the Self.

Music

Music is as old as humanity. There are versions of flutes that have been found dating back to 40,000 years ago. It appears that as soon as we had the capacity to make the instruments and the time to learn them, we wasted no time beginning to play them. And music has always had a communal aspect, which is the reason why you find music playing in many public spaces (stores, elevators, cafes and bars). It is something that we can all experience together, at once, even when individuals are alone with their thoughts and conversations are occurring between people or in groups.

What is particularly interesting about music is that even though it might be originating outside of you, it is something you can participate with. Whether it's simply tapping your foot to the beat, humming along or fully belting it out, music invites you to let go of your sense of self and your inhibitions and surrender to it. It is for this reason that music is one of the primary gateways to the Self.

Expressing Gratitude/Appreciation

One of the fastest ways to tap into the EM of Self is to find something or someone to appreciate or be grateful for. Focusing on gratitude or appreciation is effective at moving us beyond the mind because the mind is programmed to look for the next thing (and then the next thing and then the next thing) that will make us happier or improve our lot in life. But when we focus on gratitude and appreciation, it brings us immediately to **now** and to what we already have which fosters an experience of contentment. And the Self that we're referring to is always content simply having the day-to-day experience of being alive.

The gratitude/appreciation muscle is better developed in some of us than others. And, it can be easier at some times than others for all of us to focus our attention in this way. I'm well aware of those days when stopping to appreciate someone or something sounds about as appealing as a dip in the pool during a snowstorm. - But even if you have very little practice appreciating or being grateful, you can start today to great effect.

It's often easier, initially, to focus on simple ways of incorporating gratitude into your daily living. Many will say something before eating or upon waking or prior to sleeping. One way to get things jumpstarted is to consider what it would be like without something or someone in your life. For example, imagine someone you care about deeply no longer being here. Or, imagine what it would be like to not have a mobile phone. Typically, by doing this, we are able to take out blinders off and realize that the things that are already in our lives are bringing us great joy. It's as if, for a few moments at least, we just purchased that first smartphone or we've created the moment that someone we love first came into our lives.

There will be an exercise outlined at the end of the chapter to help you begin to expand your awareness of this powerful gateway to Self.

Breath

There is not a wisdom tradition that I am aware of that does not recognize the opportunity for self-realization that is inherent in paying attention to the breath. The Buddha himself attained enlightenment while focusing on his breath. Modern day spiritual leaders as diverse as Deepak Chopra, Andrew Weil, and the Dalai

Lama all speak about and teach the importance of attention to breath as a way to access higher states of consciousness.

Breath is our bridge between life and death. When you focus on your breath and nothing else, you are in intimate contact with your embodied experience. **In fact,** you are connected with the normally muted or forgotten reality that you are, at every moment, mere minutes from death if you were to stop breathing.

There are probably more breathing exercises than there are days in the year. Should you move into committed action mode (see the next chapter), you may choose to take on one of these as a regular practice. For now, there will be an exercise included in this chapter that is designed to give you a taste of what's available through breath awareness.

Dancing

Much like music, dancing has been a part of the human experience since at least the beginning of recorded history. And often, the two are intertwined. Of course, dancing takes many different forms and is done for many different reasons (ceremonial, communal, even sexual). However, what's common about all dance is that it shows us how to move beyond our minds. Whether it's a tango that hypnotizes us with the eternal interplay between masculine and feminine or a country line dance performed by hundreds moving in unison, dancing invites us to put our pride aside and risk embarrassment for the chance to feel part of something that's beyond ourselves.

Michael Jackson, a man that Guinness World Records recognizes as the most successful entertainer of all time, sums up the opportunity that dancing offers us to connect to our Self and even what's beyond that:

"On many an occasion when I am dancing, I have felt touched by something sacred. In those moments, I felt my spirit soar and become one with everything that exists. I become the stars and the moon. I become the lover and the beloved. I become the victor and the vanquished. I become the master and the slave. I become the singer and the song. I become the knower and the known. I keep on dancing and then, it is the eternal dance of creation." – From Inlay Sleeve of Dangerous (1991)

You don't have to be Michael Jackson or have his skill to

experience some of what he describes. I myself have experienced the freedom, joy and ecstasy that can be generated by even just a few minutes of freely dancing, at home, by myself. One of the exercises at the end of the chapter will delve more deeply into the opportunity that dance represents and give you some ideas for how to tap into it. And no, you won't have to register for dance classes!

Chanting/Tone

Such diverse luminaries as the inventor of the telephone, Alexander Graham Bell, self-help guru Wayne Dyer and Novel Prize winner Max Planck, among many others, talk of the idea that all matter in the universe is simply atoms vibrating at a very slow rate. They submit that the entire universe and everything in it is simply vibration happening at different frequencies.

Whether or not you subscribe to this theory, human beings have been using chanting in religious or spiritual ceremonies and tones such as "Aum" for many, many thousands of years. The fact that chanting and tone are utilized around the world in cultures that have not ever had contact with one another lends credence to the idea that there is something universal about engaging with these methods of connecting to what is beyond our mental identities.

If you've yet to participate with any kind of chanting or a yoga class where the entire class makes the sound of "Aum" at the beginning or end, you may not yet be sensitized to the unique state of mind and being that is available during or after. If nothing else, the act of matching (or attempting to match) the vibration of your voice box/larynx with those of a group of others is an activity, which necessarily brings you out of your (lower case "s") self and into the communal space. It's in that space that you begin to have access to the upper case "S" Self.

Serving Others

Finally, offering some of your time, attention or resources to others with no expectation for anything in return is a unique way to both connect you to the EM of your Self *and*, in the process benefit another or others.

Think about those times in life when it seems that no matter how hard you try or what new strategy you employ, you just can't seem to make any meaningful progress. Consider that in these times, the only thing you need to do to get to the next place in your life is to focus on how you can make a difference for others and the wider world.

I see it like a pendulum in life that swings back and forth between times of intense learning and growing that is "self centered" and times to focus on sharing what you've experienced or learned with others. Many people can relate to this cycle on a fundamental level as it relates to the period before and after having children. Ideally, one does a lot of growing and learning on their own before they feel ready to guide the life of a child. While this phenomenon happens in cycles on a longer term scale over our lifetimes, there are also many micro opportunities at various points during each and every day.

How can we recognize these opportunities? The best clue is when you catch yourself getting wrapped up in all the things that you have to do and handle and are feeling really weighed down about it. The mistake that most of us make is that when we get overwhelmed with all of the things we need to do for ourselves, we focus even more on ourselves instead of pausing to look out there. Now, I can almost hear some of you reading this exclaiming, "But I spend half my day doing things for other people!" Maybe you're shuttling multiple kids to one event or another or are taking care of ailing family members. Or maybe you're just the kind of person that is always saying yes when friends ask for your shoulder to cry on or ear to listen or mind to help them figure something out.

The thing is, there is a huge difference between doing something for someone *and* being inspired about serving that person and doing something because you "have to" or because it's expected of you. In the moments when you're feeling overwhelmed and stressed, it's almost guaranteed that you are in "have to" mode rather than inspired mode. This is not to say that expectations don't exist or that you need to always be lit up inside every time you're doing the laundry for your children. But what you can do is occasionally get yourself re–connected to the "why" behind the "what" you are doing for them.

SELF AWARENESS EXERCISES

Now that you have a broad understanding of the many ways in which you can connect to this energy magnifier of Self, let's outline some simple, powerful, and direct ways for you to give your mind a break so that you have access to what's just beyond your pre-programmed or habitual relationship with yourself, others, and the world.

Breath Exercise

Kundalini Yoga features no fewer than 1000+ different kriyas or sets of combined breath and movement exercises. As a trained Kundalini Yoga Instructor, I've chosen a basic exercise that is suitable for a beginner to Kundalini or even someone who does not practice Kundalini regularly. It's called the "Breath Awareness Exercise" and is taken from the KRI International Teacher Training Manual.

If you can situate yourself in a cross-legged pose on the floor or on a meditation cushion, that's preferable. If not, you can even do this exercise in a chair. If you are familiar with Gyan Mudra (bringing the thumb and index finger pads to touch) you can have your hands in that position. If not, simply keep your hands in prayer and place them at the center of the chest at the level of the heart.

The exercise itself can last for as little as three minutes. You'll begin by paying attention to the breath for 30 seconds or so. And then, there are just two more things for you to focus on. Bring your attention to the area between the eyebrows. Then, from there, imagine your awareness flowing from this point to a point an inch or so below the navel.

You are free to increase the length of time beyond three minutes if you desire. You can also visualize light emitting from your body and merging with the much brighter, broader light that is the cosmos or universal light.

> "We each have a unique learning style. I recommend that, if after a day or two, you are not expanding your level of awareness, you change the exercise that you are engaging with. Please refer to the Resources&References section, under the header for Chapter 5, to learn more about different learning styles."

Practice Being Grateful

There are an innumerable number of ways to increase your level of awareness of just how much there is to be grateful for in your life. I offer you three options:

1. If you sense that it would be valuable for you to interrupt the mental focus during the day, you can set a reminder in your calendar that says something like "Whisper to Yourself the Top 5 Things You Are Grateful For In This Moment." These things can be as simple as your good health, a particular friendship, or something good that's happened today or is scheduled to happen later today.

2. If you have a sense that you would do well partnering with others when it comes to learning more about this EM, you can create a list of your Top 5 choices and reach out to each of them until you find a partner. Invite them to a week-long experiment in expanding gratitude. Promise them it will be fun and the results will be surprising (because it will be and they will be!). Then, just agree to the logistics. You can text at lunchtime, email before leaving work, or have a quick phone call during the late morning. Whatever works best for the both of you! The idea is the same...to identify the top 5 things you are grateful for in this moment.

3. If you're the kind of person that benefits from reviewing the day that's just passed, consider keeping a mini gratitude journal for a week. You can leave it by your bedside, or, if you are someone who tends to need a little extra nudge to stay on track with a new activity, you can even store it in your pillowcase so that there's no way you'll forget to do it.

Heart First

If you enjoy doing something physical and fun to connect with Self, this one's for you. The idea is for you to find some way during your day to get your heart above your brain. You may not be aware of it, but your heart actually has upwards of 40,000 neurons and releases its own peptides that interact with the endocrine system to produce hormones. While I can't point to any science that proves the benefits of getting the heart above the head, what I've observed for myself is that it's one of the fastest and simplest ways of shifting my mental state when I'm in need of a burst of inspiration or simply a change in the tone of my thinking.

You can choose from a wide array of options to accomplish this task. That said, I strongly recommend that you check with your doctor before engaging with these suggestions to ensure your health will not be negatively impacted. If you are not very flexible or have some limitations in the physical body, you can simply stand with your feet hip distance apart and reach your fingers towards your toes with your neck relaxed. Another option is to lie down on the floor with your feet planted and then lift your hips up for 30–60 seconds, keeping your head and neck on the floor.

If you're feeling fit and have checked with your doctor, you can play with some handstands against the wall. There are also some more creative and fun ways to achieve the same result. You may have noticed an apparatus that allows you to place your feet into a bar that fits in a doorway that allows you to hang upside down like a bat. You can also try cartwheels and somersaults if you're feeling particularly frisky!

It's Not About You

In this exercise you are going to consciously do or say something with the intention of either bringing joy to another human being or bolstering their belief in the basic goodness of the universe or humanity.

The expression of this exercise can range from the simple act of giving your seat to someone else on a crowded train to sending a text to someone to let them know that you're thinking of them and to share something specific that you appreciate about them.

The only rule with this method of connecting to Self is that it must be genuine. It can never be a "should," as in, "My culture tells me I *should* give my seat on a train to a woman if one is standing." It has to come from a true appreciation for the fact that we have the capacity in any given moment to improve the experience of life for others with our words or actions.

I'm going to refrain from providing too many examples here as the opportunities to engage with this exercise become very obvious and numerous once you begin genuinely looking for opportunities.

Music Break!

This one goes just as you imagine it would. By now many of you will have seen an example of the type of flash mob where a large group of people have pre-planned to come to a certain place at a set time and begin dancing, singing, or performing all at once. Well, this exercise does not have to be as elaborate as all of that.

All you need to do is choose whether it's going to be a music/singing break or a music/dancing break. I know people who are totally comfortable singing or dancing while walking down the street and you may want to give that a try. If not, at any point in the day when you find yourself alone for a couple of minutes, press play on the song that is most reliable to make you feel good, crank up the volume (use headsets if you are concerned about disturbing the neighbors) and belt or shake it out! It really is as simple as that.

What you are doing is celebrating the fact that you're alive and expressing yourself with wild abandon. You are connecting with the thousands and maybe millions of other souls who have ever been touched by the song that you're listening to.

Prayer/Chanting

What is prayer when we distill it to its essence? Well, first, we are acknowledging that there is a power beyond ourselves that is at work in the universe. We're also having faith that this power can be a benign force for good and that it might respond to the desires of us mortals.

There is no one particular way to pray. Sometimes I sit cross-legged on the ground with my hands on my knees and simply close my eyes and envision a person I want to pray for. In these instances, I might even imagine myself traveling to where I think they might be and beam white light in their general direction.

Softly chanting a mantra is a great way to deliver you into a state of heightened awareness so that you can formulate a prayer that is as lucid and clear as possible. An easy one to begin with which includes the "Aum" sound we discussed earlier in the chapter is "Om Namah Shivaya." This is a Sanskrit mantra that basically means "adoration to Shiva," one of the primary gods in Hinduism.

After you have chanted for two or three minutes, in the silence that follows, allow your prayer to form and then send it out in all directions.

Not Right Now, But Later, Yes!

There's one final exercise option for those who, perhaps, are so busy during their day that they can't even imagine engaging with any of the previous exercises that have been outlined. Or, maybe you don't yet feel comfortable dancing, chanting or getting your heart above your head in public.

This one is all about exploring the opportunities that exist for you to set aside a bit of time in the next week to create the conditions necessary for you to properly connect with the EM of Self. All you'll need is your calendar and possibly an Internet-enabled device. If you are already aware of an activity that you can engage with on your own that is likely to give you access to "being in the flow" and following your intuition or heart, then schedule it in your calendar when you can see it would work for you.

If you're not sure about what kind of activity to engage with, it can be something as simple as taking 20 or 30 minutes to walk, in no particular direction and with no particular plan, through a park or along a beach. Or, if you live in a city, taking a walk and listening for music that calls to you and stopping to watch a street performer or popping into a bar or jazz club for a bit. You could even just take a walk around a particular neighborhood on a search for some public art to take in.

Whatever you do, the main idea is for you to not have it all planned out beforehand. You want to open yourself up to the rhythm of life around you and allow your thinking and planning mind to take the back seat while your Self comes to the forefront. Go on, I dare you!

Remember, these exercises are my best suggestions for dealing directly with the energetic magnifiers. You are welcome to leverage exercises or modalities that you are already familiar with, search out new ones, or create your own! For the most up-to-date thinking on all of these exercises and to share your experience or get support, you can head over to www.consciousliving.ning.com to register for access to the online community.

CHAPTER 9

COMMITTED ACTION MODE

If you've been reading this book linearly thus far, this chapter marks an important milestone. For the rest of the book, we are no longer so focused on discovering new things about each of the EMs. Instead, I'm now assuming you have a sufficient level of clarity about what works and does not work for you in relating to each of these EMs and you can see the benefit in fully engaging with certain practices on a regular basis. This is not merely a conceptual shift in focus or understanding. In all previous chapters of the book, the tone and approach has been one of careful attention and curiosity. The tone and approach for the next several chapters is one of consistent focus and determination.

As a guideline, I suggest that you engage with the One Week Satisfaction Booster (Chapter 4) process a minimum of two or three times (focused on the same area of life), prior to seriously engaging with the remainder of this book. Of course, this is not to say that you won't get value from reading this chapter and the following ones. What I am suggesting is that, in order to create the conditions for sustainable, committed action, it's important that you have sufficient awareness of the Energy Magnifiers and how to engage with them. Jumping immediately into committed action mode would be a little bit like deciding to run a marathon and then starting out your training by attempting to run a full one the first time you run.

One final caveat to the caveat above. ;) If you are someone who has had a fair amount of experience in awareness mode via other modalities or transformational growth experiences in one tradition or another, do feel free to dive right in here. Then, if you notice that you are not able to maintain the consistency required to see the results you want, consider heading to Chapter 3 to work through that material before re-visiting this chapter.

In this mode, it's all about creating new behavior patterns, new ways of thinking and readdressing some of how you spend your time. This will require a more sustained effort. When engaging with this portion of the journey toward increasing you baseline for life satisfaction, there will be many opportunities and seemingly good reasons to give up or take detours. In order to minimize the risk of this happening and to support you in generating a sustainable shift in your lived experience, there are several key concepts that must be understood and applied.

Identifying Purpose

Part of why it's so important to spend a sufficient amount of time in awareness mode is that getting really clear about the parts of your life that are not working for you (and what exactly has been standing in the way of true satisfaction in your life) quite naturally leads to a greater degree of certainty about what you **do** want your life to look like.

For some people, the simple act of finally seeing clearly where they're at in awareness mode is so fundamentally disturbing/ motivating that they have all the fuel they need to propel them into committed action mode with gusto. This is more likely to be the case if it's one of the first times that someone is consciously addressing their level of life satisfaction.

But this is not always the case. And so, it's important to develop a strong relationship with where you're headed and why you are heading there. It's critical that you are lit up, inspired, and energized by the mere thought of what you intend to accomplish. I've found that coming back to the EM's at this juncture can be a great help.

How do we deal with the fact that different people are motivated by different things in life? Well, if you are savvy about the Energy Magnifiers, you can determine which one is most abundant for you and tap into that as you create clarity around your purpose and cultivate the motivation to move purposefully toward your desired outcome.

You are probably aware that there are some people for whom the meaning of life exists in their emotional experience. They do well when they envision or allow themselves to experience what they'll be feeling and how intensely they'll be feeling it when they reach their goal or realize the outcome they desire.

For others, tapping into the EM of the Self provides the necessary "juice" that infuses them with a sense of purpose. It's when they consider what their particular gifts are and what the over-arching theme of their life is that they are invigorated to summon the discipline and courage it will take to stay the course.

Still others do well to logically and methodically map out the measurable specifics of exactly what life will look like when they have shifted what they see needs shifting. These people are tapping into the EM of the mind.

A relatively simple way to begin plugging in to your personal purpose recipe exists. Let's start by taking a look from several different angles at why you are up for making a fundamental change. So, we can pause and dive into that now. Simply fill in the blank for the following four statements (in pencil):

○ At the end of this period of growth and change on my life journey, I will feel _____.

○ At the end of this period of growth and change on my life journey, I will now be able to _____.

○ At the end of this period of growth and change on my life journey, I will have achieved the following specific, measurable outcomes: _____

○ While this period of growth and change on my life's journey will be challenging at times, I will stick with it because I know that the real purpose behind this period of growth and change is: _____.

Now, go back and read the full sentences out loud. After reading each sentence, give it a rating on a scale from one to ten. One represents very little inspiration and aliveness after having read it and 10 signifies you are almost jumping out of your seat with excitement to get started.

You may find that there is more than one statement that warrants a high mark. Or, you may find that no one statement yields a particularly high rating and that you need to find a way to combine two or more statements into a coherent amalgamation that somehow taps into multiple aspects of this future vision. Feel free to use these building block statements in different combinations or stitch together multiple pieces into the fabric of your personalized purpose.

While you may not settle on the perfect purpose statement right now, what's important is that you continually bring your attention to your purpose during the course of your engagement with this material in committed action mode. Oftentimes, the source of the lack of action or progress can be traced back to something that's missing in the "why" you started off on this leg of the journey in the first place.

Making it Tangible

Now that you've begun to outline the overall purpose of your committed action, it's important to be as clear and descriptive as possible about the experience, outcome or result you desire.

Many people have a less than empowered relationship with goal setting. Sometimes, we resist setting a goal for fear of not reaching it and being disappointed. And sometimes we don't set goals because we have failed so many times in the past to reach them that we think to ourselves "What's the point?" Nonetheless, without a clear goal, we are akin to a ship at sea without the guidance of a compass or the stars.

One of the most important aspects of goal setting, much like being clear on your purpose, is to ensure that your goals "speak" to you in a way that you can hear. You are looking for the right mix of emotional urgency, mental clarity, and soulful connection to be present in any goal that you are setting. In addition, it's important that the goal is conceived so clearly that it allows you to objectively know when you have reached it. What I have found over my years of coaching is that people's experience of satisfaction in life is strongly correlated with the frequency with which they are able to identify and then experience reaching specific, measurable goals.

It can be very helpful to create a first draft of your goal(s) and then ask yourself (or have someone else ask you) the following questions. I was inspired to create them as a result of the coaching and guidance I received from Marilena Minucci, who is, in turn, inspired by George T. Doran's paper, "There's a S.M.A.R.T. way to write management's goals and objectives." You may know of S.M.A.R.T. goal setting via Peter Drucker, as he is generally credited with having popularized their use as part of his "management by objectives" approach.

S.M.A.R.T. has been interpreted many ways but typically stands for Specific, Measurable, Attainable or Achievable, Realistic or Relevant and Time-bound.

Questions to Support You In **Creating Goals that Get Reached**:

○ By when do you say you will have reached this goal?

○ How does this goal reflect or relate to your broader purpose at this time in your life?

○ Is there anything that you can see you need to do to create sufficient time or energy to do what it takes to achieve this goal? (This can include letting people know what you are up to, so that they understand why you may not be as available as you normally are for a while or asking others for support or even ending your participation with other things in life that are not as important as reaching your goal).

○ Does this goal capture exactly what you want? Is there any way you could make it even more real for you?

○ How would an outside observer know that you have reached this goal in physical reality? (This is important, even for goals that deal with your internal state).

I've noticed that spending a bit more time up front, in the goal creation process, significantly shortens the time it takes to reach a goal. Often, when we don't take the time to get very clear up front, the goal will tend to shift and change as we head toward it, which can create confusion and also contribute to a loss of momentum or commitment to its realization.

Remaining Empowered

Now that you've gotten empowered with your purpose and created a clear goal, the train is leaving the station and you're headed to your destination. One of the fastest ways to stray off course and end up somewhere far from where you wanted to go on your journey toward a specific goal is to begin breaking your word to yourself. By this, I mean committing to something and then not actually following through with it or, even worse, not even acknowledging that you broke your word. In other modes, you can get away with this to some extent. But in committed action mode you are, indeed, committed. And commitment comes with many rewards but also requires an increased level of accountability to what you promise to yourself and to others.

When you are in committed action mode, you will be regularly engaging with the Energy Magnifiers and this will mean spending a fair bit of time in ways that you haven't before. Because you will be taking on deepening certain practices, it will require you to make promises to yourself and keep your word to yourself.

I have to give a shout out to Landmark Education at this juncture in the book. My training at that organization over the course of three years was an experience that forever shifted my relationship with myself and with the words that come out of my mouth. What I not only learned but also experienced on a day-to-day basis, is the absolute necessity of maintaining a powerful relationship with what I promise, both to myself **and** others. I also saw how the results I achieved were made possible by either following through on what I'd promised or getting to the source of what got in the way so I can have a reasonable expectation that I will follow through the next time I make a promise.

As far as other people are concerned, besides your actions, your ability to honor your word is the most important indicator that you are a person that adds value to the world. When you demonstrate that you do what you say you will (or own and clean up the mess when you don't), it has a direct impact on how others view you and brings opportunities that would not otherwise be available.

But perhaps more important than these external benefits, learning how to honor your word also directly empowers **you.** When you know that when you give your word to something, it will actually happen, you are empowered. While we have control over almost nothing in life, being able to really and truly trust yourself when you give your word to some action or to some**one** does feel about as close as it gets to feeling "in control" in this lifetime. While you won't always keep your word, if you almost always honor it, the results are that you know with almost 100% certainty that what comes out of your mouth will become reality. This is power.

There is one other critical piece of the puzzle when it comes to remaining empowered. It's important that when you do break your word with yourself (and you will!), that you 1) treat yourself with compassion and 2) make a new promise. In fact, this one-two step is an important part of the process in this mode. When you commit to fundamentally shifting how you are operating in an area of your life, you will stumble regularly, especially at the beginning. It's actually how you know that you are making real change.

A Kick In The Pants

Some people out there make a decision to, say, quit smoking or become a vegetarian and then actually do it and never look back. You may be this kind of person or know someone like it. And really, to varying degrees, we all have at least some capacity to create a change and maintain that change on our own.

But for many people, most of the time, we are more likely to reach our highest goals with at least some external support. In addition to the benefit of having someone to share the experience of this part of your personal journey with in detail, you can empower this person to support you in honoring your word to yourself.

I've coached many people who had said to themselves (inside their head) that they would make a change but didn't make that change. I've also coached many people who have told other people in their life that they were going to make a change and then didn't make that change. What I have seen makes the most difference in the likelihood that you will make a change is having someone else to "report to" about your progress. I've been told countless times, by those I coach, that one of the aspects of coaching that they appreciate most is knowing that they will be speaking with me on a regular basis and that I'm going to ask them about their progress with the action steps they created the previous time we met.

You can set up this kind of accountability in many ways. Sometimes, you'll want some additional support from an individual who is trained and experienced in guiding people toward new levels of presence in their lives on a one-on-one basis. At other times, having a community of people who are all focused on a particular type of self-development or shifting a particular aspect of their life is the perfect recipe for support. I've also witnessed the powerful results that can occur when two people choose to trade support with one another.

Whether it's with someone you are paying to coach you, someone you are trading services with or a group program, what is critical when entering into an accountability relationship is that you open yourself up to the support. What does it look like? It looks like being willing to fail sometimes. It looks like being vulnerable and open to input and guidance. And, it looks like being willing to make big promises and stretch yourself to reach them.

What Makes You Tick – Part 1

So, you've got your purpose, you've got your goals, you're keeping yourself empowered and you have figured out what kind of support you require to make steady progress. But something is still "off." Perhaps you are making progress, but not as quickly as you like. Or perhaps you are in a "two steps forward, one step back" dance and your legs are starting to get tired. If this is the case, there is a dynamic that may be at play that is slowing your progress or making the process more complicated than it needs to be.

As we discussed earlier, sometimes we make change more quickly and easily than at other times. Consider that this occurrence was not completely random and that there was a way that you were living that you may have been unconscious about. I have personally utilized a powerful model for understanding how human beings go about making change for the past 5+ years. It's called the Triad of Change, created by Dr. Donald Epstein and it offers a simple yet profound way for people to maximize change while minimizing struggle.

The full application of the deep wisdom of this model is beyond the scope of this book. That said, you can utilize one core element that can be incredibly powerful in assisting you to optimize the way you make change. It's based on the awareness that there are three critical elements that make up both every change you've ever made in your life *and* that are operating in every area of your life. And, most importantly, that you can choose how you are focusing your attention on these elements to maximize your rate of progress.

The first element is the realm of your thoughts and feelings. You are always having thoughts and feelings about the different areas of your life. And, when a change occurs, you had one view on (or experience of) an area of your life before the change, and another after. Whether you are focusing on or dwelling in your thoughts and feeling is a choice.

The second element is the way things are organized or set up. In order for any change you make to be sustainable, there is something that has to physically shift in the way your life is set up. Again here, you can spend time focused on the way things are set up (or the way they're not) or you can focus on one of the other two aspects.

The third is that your behavior changed. That is, there was some activity you were engaged with before (or there was some lack of activity), and then after the change the previous behavior shifted or a new one began **and** was sustainable. In every area of life, there is a certain set of actions you are taking and ones that you are not taking (whether you are aware you could take them or not) As with the previous two elements, you can focus in on the actions or you can focus on one or both of the other elements.

What is critical for you to notice if you are truly interested in generating a change (and doing it with an abundance of energy) is that there is one of these three elements that, when you focus on it for too long, will sabotage the effort that you are making.

Let's take the example of someone who wants to be in a committed relationship. This person is always going on and on about which bar or social event and what the perfect time is to arrive so that they increase the odds of meet their soul mate. They're regularly focusing in on the logistics of when and where and not paying much attention to their actions when they are actually in situations where they are meeting potential mates **or** the thoughts and feelings they are having in those situations. If this person was aware of the fact that all of their focus on where and when was just one piece of the puzzle (and the piece that is least effective for them to focus on), they would be able to switch their attention and spend more of their time and energy taking a look at what they're doing and what they're thinking and feeling before, during, and after these events.

For a different person in the same situation, it could be completely different. For them, they may be so caught up in the thinking and feeling about being in a relationship (or not being in one) that they never actually pay any attention to putting themselves in the right places at the right times. Another person may be so focused on their actions or the actions that others are taking (or not taking) and neglecting the whole realm of thoughts/feeling and when/where.

So, when you find that you are struggling in committed action mode (and you will), I recommend that you check in to see which of the three aspects currently has the majority of your attention and then consciously shift it up so that you are spending more of your time focused on the other two aspects. As you engage with this tool further, you will begin to learn which of the three is the most reliable change agent for you and which one is most reliable for getting in your way.

What Makes You Tick – Part Two

Another important dynamic to be aware of in committed action mode is the balance you strike along the spectrum of being fully and totally engaged with yourself and **your** process vs. being engaged with the outer world and stimulated by the influence of other people. Some people exist on the far ends of this spectrum. There are those that do best when left almost completely to their own devices to focus and work though whatever they are digging into and transforming in their lives. Others are at the other end and only do well with making a change if they are in near constant communication with and engagement with other people's ideas or some external process that they can follow.

As you engage in this process of materially shifting an area of your life in committed action mode, you'll begin to be sensitized to where you operate best along this spectrum. Many of the exercises in this book will tend to pull you inward and this may be a bit overwhelming for some, especially at first. If you find this happening, I recommend you find a partner to come along for the self-development ride with you so you can share with and support one another. There can be great value in getting out of your own experience and diving into another's for a bit.

This is not quite the same as our earlier discussion about getting support in the "Kick in the Pants" section. What we're looking at here is whether you're with yourself or others when you're **actually engaged** with exercises or modalities that are supporting you in shifting an area of your life.

Switch It Up

There's one final potential roadblock as you travel toward your destination of a significant and lasting shift in a particular area of your life. It has to do with getting attached to or rigid about a particular outcome. Oftentimes, when we create a goal and begin moving toward it, the actual experience of taking the actions toward that goal can alter the goal itself. In fact, the awareness mode that we looked at earlier in the book hasn't ended. It's now part and parcel of the committed action mode you are in and new awareness can come up at any moment, which can alter your trajectory.

When this happens, don't be afraid to switch up the particular exercises or modalities that you're engaged with, as long as the end goal of a shifted daily living experience in an area of life that is important to you remains the focus. It's not about rigidity, but instead a consistent focus and a sensitivity and responsiveness to new learning. Even though you already know enough to know that changes need to be made and have identified ways to go about doing that, allow yourself the flexibility to find what works best for you in reaching your final destination.

There's just one more conversation to have before we dive into the specific Energy Magnifiers. Let's talk a bit about what kind of time commitment it's going to take to fully and sustainably shift your current patterns of thinking or behaving. I want to be completely up front with you about what you're in for so that you are clear and empowered from the beginning. What we're not talking about here in Committed Action mode is some kind of short-term exploration or quick fix. Many thousands of self-help books already promise you everything from a dream body to the perfect marriage to a clutter-free house in less than 10, 7 or even 5 days. While I can't say whether or not any of those books or methods will deliver results for you, I can say that I'm promising you nothing of the sort. ☺

In my experience coaching thousands of people, the place for these shorter time frame explorations and engagements is back in awareness mode, where we utilized one-week long satisfaction boosters. It's appropriate, when you are just beginning to get clear on how you've been operating, for you to take 7 days to bring your attention to an issue with a particular area of life. However, when we try to shoe horn in sustainable change into such a short time frame, something's got to give. And so, what ends up happening is one of two things. If the program is very intensive, you're likely to cut corners and/or not see it through to the end of whatever timeframe is being promised. Or, you will see it through and get the result, only to set yourself up for disappointment because you haven't learned how to sustain the change much beyond the initial timeframe.

In committed action mode, we're actually interested in shifting an area of your life and/or your relationship with one or more of your Energy Magnifiers for a sustainable and lengthy period of time. In fact, if you engage with committed action mode fully, it's very likely that the area of your life you are focused on and your relationship with the Energy Magnifier(s) will never be the same again. This is the promise that I am making to you.

In order for this to occur, you're simply going to need to spend more than 5, 7 or 14 days consistently engaged in this mode. Now, there are many different experts and schools of thought with varying ideas about *exactly how long* it takes for a person to sustainably replace an existing unwanted habitual way of being or acting with a new, desired one.

I have personally participated with multiple modalities and successfully (and sustainably) shifted my own fundamental patterns of behavior and thinking, generating unforeseen and remarkable shifts in my life. And what I have noticed is that, well, the timeframe varies. I have participated in 3-month-long self development courses, 40-day meditation series, and 30-day yoga challenges. I've also been trained in guiding people through a 6-month program to transform their relationship to their health and nutrition. And with each of these, I can confirm that a result was achieved and sustained well beyond the initial timeframe. So, where does that leave us?

If we look at what the scientific world has to say about it, research done at University College London and published in the European Journal of Social Psychology found that, on average, it takes 66 days for a person to generate a totally new automatic behavior pattern. Of course, this is an *average* only, and the number of days will vary widely depending upon you, the behavior you want to shift and the already existing life circumstances you have. And, of course, we are dealing here with not just a habit, but actually positively impacting your experience of satisfaction in an entire area of life. So, what's important to get here is that fundamental change **will** take some time *and* it **will** happen (if you stick to it).

There was one more finding from the research that is particularly relevant for us at this critical juncture when you are moving from awareness into committed action. The study showed that even those that missed a day every now and then on the road to forming a new habit were able to successfully create the new habit. What does this mean for you? It's a reminder of the fact that what's more important than perfection is persistence when it comes to making fundamental and long sought after changes in life. Given this finding, you might consider creating a post-it or weekly reminder on your digital device that says something along the lines of "Persistence Trumps Perfection" to help keep you inspired as you move through committed action mode.

Would you like some additional support in the form of a tracking document that will help you stay on top of your actions with the various EM's over time? Head on over to the website at www. consciousliving.ning.com and request it.

Now that you're aware of the building blocks and nature of committed action mode, it's time to re-visit the individual Energy Magnifiers with the intention to leverage them for all they're worth. This will be an exciting, sometimes challenging and ultimately very rewarding period of time for you if you are truly ready to generate the shifts you want to make in your life!

CHAPTER 10

A WELL-OILED MACHINE

I f you're reading this chapter, I am assuming you are in one of two places. One may be that you have already spent a fair bit of time with some of the exercises outlined in Chapter 4 regarding the Energy Magnifier of the body. Now you find yourself at the point where you are interested in designing, and then committing to, a deeper and longer-lasting relationship with your physical needs and capacities.

The other place you could be is that you have come to this book with an already high level of awareness about what works for you when it comes to engaging with your body. However, you may not have discovered how to stick to a regular engagement with it. In other words, you've got the "know-how" but not the "will-do."

Whichever place you are in, this chapter will support you in engaging with the various dynamics and underlying rhythms that are important to understand as you develop a durable yet flexible habit of body connection.

In this lifetime, we are capable of experiencing so much learning, growth and evolution. We may live in many different places, get to know many thousands of people and accumulate (and get rid of) countless possessions. But only one thing will be with you for the entire ride: your body. If you desire the fullest expression of your life's potential, you will want to develop a way that works for you to take exquisite care of this earthly vessel. After all, it's the only one you're going to get this go around.

To best illustrate how interacting with the Energy Magnifier of Body differs in Committed Action mode relative to Awareness mode, let's re-visit the "mini-magnifiers" for body that we initially discussed in Chapter 4. If you recall, the Energy Magnifier of Body is actually a three-legged stool that requires answers to three questions:

- What's Going In?
- Is it Strong and Supple?
- Are You Loving It Up?

What you're now looking for is what you can commit to engaging with (and how you'll do that), for each of these mini-magnifiers, for an extended period of time (six weeks or more).

In order to provide some structure for generating a plan that is both rigorous and flexible, I've created the following worksheet to help guide you. (You can use pencil, if you like.)

Week One

Nutrition

New Item(s) I'm Adding In To My Weekly Diet: _____

Frequency: _____

Quantity: _____

Other/Notes: _____

Exercise

What I'm Adding In/Changing: _____

Frequency: _____

Duration: _____

Other/Notes: _____

Self Care

What I'm Giving To Myself: _____

Frequency: _____

Duration: _____

Other/Notes: _____

Week Two

What I Learned From The Prior Week Is: _____

_____

What I Will Alter Based On That Learning Is: _____

_____

Nutrition

New Item(s) I'm Adding In To My Weekly Diet: _____

Frequency: _____

Quantity: _____

Other/Notes: _____

Exercise

What I'm Adding In/Changing: _____

Frequency: _____

Duration: _____

Other/Notes: _____

Self Care

What I'm Giving To Myself: _____

Frequency: _____

Duration: _____

Other/Notes: _____

Week Three

What I Learned From The Prior Week Is: _____

_____

What I Will Alter Based On That Learning Is: _____

_____

Nutrition

New Item(s) I'm Adding In To My Weekly Diet: _____

Frequency: _____

Quantity: _____

Other/Notes: _____

Exercise

What I'm Adding In/Changing: _____

Frequency: _____

Duration: _____

Other/Notes: _____

Self Care

What I'm Giving To Myself: _____

Frequency: _____

Duration: _____

Other/Notes: _____

Week Four

What I Learned From The Prior Week Is: _____

_____

What I Will Alter Based On That Learning Is: _____

_____

Nutrition

New Item(s) I'm Adding In To My Weekly Diet: _____

Frequency: _____

Quantity: _____

Other/Notes: _____

Exercise

What I'm Adding In/Changing: _____

Frequency: _____

Duration: _____

Other/Notes: _____

Self Care

What I'm Giving To Myself: _____

Frequency: _____

Duration: _____

Other/Notes: _____

Week Five

What I Learned From The Prior Week Is: _____

_____

What I Will Alter Based On That Learning Is: _____

_____

Nutrition

New Item(s) I'm Adding In To My Weekly Diet: _____

Frequency: _____

Quantity: _____

Other/Notes: _____

Exercise

What I'm Adding In/Changing: _____

Frequency: _____

Duration: _____

Other/Notes: _____

Self Care

What I'm Giving To Myself: _____

Frequency: _____

Duration: _____

Other/Notes: _____

Week Six

What I Learned From The Prior Week Is: _____

_____

What I Will Alter Based On That Learning Is: _____

_____

Nutrition

New Item(s) I'm Adding In To My Weekly Diet: _____

Frequency: _____

Quantity: _____

Other/Notes: _____

Exercise

What I'm Adding In/Changing: _____

Frequency: _____

Duration: _____

Other/Notes: _____

Self Care

What I'm Giving To Myself: _____

Frequency: _____

Duration: _____

Other/Notes: _____

Head to www.consciousliving.ning.com for a soft copy of this worksheet.

How To Use this Worksheet

One of the most important aspects of operating successfully in committed action mode is learning from the experience and making adjustments as you go. To that end, I've included prompts for this awareness at the beginning of each week's plan.

With nutrition, I recommend adding in no more than one new food item at a time. There are multiple reasons for this. First, making one change at a time allows you to measure the impact on your system. Generally speaking, it takes at least two to three days to begin to register a difference in your energy or mood after having made a dietary change. So, adding in two foods per week can work, as long as you space them out.

It also gives you the experience of successfully making a shift rather than overwhelming yourself with multiple changes at one time, increasing the risk of unsuccessfully maintaining the shift. Remember, what you're at work on here is fundamentally shifting a behavior pattern. What's far more important than the size of the change is the sustainability of it. Also, it's not always just about adding a particular food item in. Sometimes it's about committing to an increased number of meals per week that you are preparing yourself or that are 100% unprocessed, for example.

When it comes to exercise, the same principle applies with regard to not making too many changes at once. In addition, I recommend that you start with relatively few numbers of days per week and relative short duration exercise initially. You can always increase both in subsequent weeks.

Finally, with self-care, if this is entirely new terrain for you, I recommend you begin by just giving yourself five minutes every couple of days where you close your eyes and bring your attention to your breath. If you have the time and space, lying down while doing this will intensify the benefits as you will be able to let all of your muscles relax completely.

Some people may find it helpful to start with just one of the three mini-magnifiers the first week, and then layer in another the second or third week, and so on. If you do take that approach, you will want to increase the number of total weeks to accommodate for the extra time taken by the gentler start.

There is one further dynamic to be aware of as you fully engage in committed action mode for the Energy Magnifier of the body. As you take on new and varied behaviors and begin disrupting the existing flow you've been in, there are bound to be ebbs and flows in what your body is calling for from day to day and sometimes even during the same day. So, allow yourself some flexibility to honor what you are feeling. If you don't exercise when you said you would or you miss a day of eating dark leafy greens, forgive yourself immediately and turn the page. Slip-ups never ruin progress but giving up when you slip up does! If I miss a day of eating greens, I simply double up the next day. Or, sometimes if I don't feel good about strength training in the morning, I'll re-schedule it for the evening or double up the next day.

In order to begin identifying your focus for week one, we'll be re-visiting the exercises that we first considered back in the body awareness chapter. These will include a more complete outline of dietary changes, physical exercises to consider, and various options for self-care. Reviewing these exercises will allow you to complete the worksheet each week in the way that makes the most sense for you at this time in your life *and* at that point in your journey through Committed Action mode.

BODY EXERCISE UPGRADES

Way back in Chapter 5, when we were exploring the body in awareness mode, I shared with you some specific exercises that would begin to expand your awareness. Now that you are in Committed Action mode, we'll take a look at how to deepen some of the awareness practices. In some cases, this simply means extending the practice for a longer period of time or for a longer duration. In other cases there are

"We each have a unique learning style. I recommend that, if after a day or two, you are not expanding your level of awareness, you change the exercise that you are engaging with. Please refer to the Resources&References section, under the header for Chapter 5, to learn more about different learning styles."

some modifications to the exercise itself.

Before we dive in to the exercise upgrades, this is a good time to remind you of our discussion in the previous chapter about setting up accountability for yourself. In fact, you may also benefit from taking it a step further and seeking out coaching and support from those who have been down the road of committed action before you and who can guide you as you set out to design your action plan. I say this now, not to suggest that you don't have the capacity to create your own plan, but rather to offer you an option that will very likely speed up your progress through this mode and result in less struggle as you move toward your goals. As a starting off point, if you're not sure where to look first, you can always head to www.consciousliving.ning.com and see what group or individual support is currently available.

Remember, the following exercises are designed to be jumping off points and thought starters for you. For many people, having these existing exercises outlined here is exactly what they need to plug in to for entering Committed Action mode. For others, it's going to be important that you either make the exercises your own by modifying them in some way or that you create your own, based on what you learned back in Awareness Mode. As you move through the weeks, and most importantly as you come toward the end of the length of time you have committed yourself in this mode, open yourself up to inspiration and insight into how to modify the exercises you are engaged with so that they fit the evolving experience.

All right! Let's jump in to the deep end and re-visit the Energy Magnifier of the body.

Cardio/Strength

Over the course of my lifetime I've visited Committed Action mode many times with a wide variety of different physical exercises.

These have included everything from lifting weights to stationary bike to swimming to high intensity interval training. My firm belief is that, as long as you are not in danger of injuring yourself (it's always a good idea to have some kind of outside guidance when you begin engaging with a new type of exercise), it's not as important which exercise you choose to engage with at the moment, as long as you do actually choose and commit to one.

If you're looking for some inspiration around all of the different ways you can strengthen your muscles or your cardio-vascular system, have a look at www.fitnessblender.com. At last count, they were featuring at least nine different modes of exercise that you can explore. Simply choose the one that seems the most appropriate or interesting for you as you begin and then be open to switching things up as the weeks go by.

Another fun way to approach this is to take a minute or two to write down all the different ways you enjoyed using your body in your younger years (before the age of, say, 12). Identify all the different activities you enjoyed and then describe how it used to make you feel or why you loved it. This can provide some inspiration as you re-approach your body as an adult.

Focusing On The Breath

There is certainly no shortage of breathwork modalities to choose from. If you are not necessarily interested in a deeper exploration of Pranayama, T'ai Chi, Qigong or one of the many modern modalities, you can simply take the exercise we explored back in Chapter 5 and gradually extend it in duration and practice over the entire length of this committed action phase.

You may also choose to increase the amount of times during the day that you are checking in with your breath. This can be achieved by setting reminders for yourself or appending the practice to existing events that you know occur each and every day for you (after brushing your teeth, prior to eating, etc.).

Taking Pampering to The Next Level

If you explored this back in Awareness Mode, you know how wonderful it can feel to give to yourself "just because." When it comes to Committed Action mode, it's all about find the rhythm that works for you. For me, I set a task in my digital devices that reminds me once a week to look back and ensure that I have, at least once, pampered myself in some way. In the beginning, my concept of pampering was limited to either a bath or a facial, but has since expanded to include all kinds of activities (a nap at the pool, restorative yoga, etc.). In reality, there is no "right way" to pamper yourself. It's about the state of being that you generate; it's about being deserving in the best possible meaning of the word. It's about being both the giver and receiver of a gift at the same time. And, if you're looking for a fun (and interactive) way to pamper yourself, try having 10 hugs (of at least 10 seconds each) in one day!

The 12 Stages of Healing

In more than one chapter I have outlined for you different exercises from a modality called Somato Respiratory Integration (SRI), of which I have been a facilitator for many thousands of people. I have personally used the modality for the better part of a decade to engage more deeply with my own body and to better understand how the rest of the Energy Magnifiers influence (and are influenced by) it. If you have enjoyed your experience with SRI or are interested in diving deeper into its many gifts, one way to do this in Committed Action mode is to make your way through the workbook that is available. It's an illustrated, practical guide to each of the exercises and provides ample background as to the consciousness associated with each exercise. It also includes relevant questions that will help deepen your experience. I've listed where you can find the workbook in the Resources chapter at the end of the book.

Becoming Plastic Man (or Woman!)

If you enjoyed the mini stretch break back in Chapter 5, consider that it's time to gradually build a yoga practice. Much like the many options available when it comes to strength training and cardio, the last decade or so has given us an explosion of options for yoga. For those that like it intense and regimented, you could practice Bikram Yoga (the same 26 poses in nearly 105 degree Fahrenheit heat for 90 minutes). If you want to be able to flow more smoothly and easily in your body, there are super gentle and flowing 30-minute classes that incorporate elements of rhythmic dance.

And, you don't have the excuse any longer of not being close to a studio or a skillful teacher. Many high quality services online allow you to take the perfect class for you in any moment. You can choose a class based on the amount of time you have, the type of yoga you prefer, the teacher and even a specific body part. You can even take a class based on a life circumstance, such as after a day of travel or yoga to start your day with more energy. For a recommendation on a particular service that I've been using, check out the Resources list in the back of the book.

Cleaning Out The Inbox – Version 2.0

You may recall that one of the awareness exercises included a one-week period of either adding various things in to your diet or being more mindful of what's going in and how it's going in. Now, in Committed Action mode, we're going to broaden the mix of possible adjustments. Again, I want to emphasize that these exercises are designed as jumping off points. While there's much you will eventually figure out on your own (or that you can find information about online), nothing can replace the guidance of a trained and experienced health coach or holistically minded nutritionist or dietician.

Beyond the lemon water, dark greens, unprocessed food and chewing awareness that we've already touched on in Chapter 5, the following list is designed to provide some additional option for focus during this longer term effort to transform how and what you are eating:

Protein – There are two primary aspects of protein consumption to consider:
➤ First, where are you along the spectrum of % of total calories that you are currently getting from protein? You may have already been out of balance with your personal requirements prior to moving into Committed Action mode **or** due to other changes you are now making to your level of exercise, you may require more than you did before.
➤ Second, what mixture of protein sources are you currently tapping into and does a re-balancing need to occur? Protein is

available from sources as diverse as animal meat, eggs, seafood, nuts, seeds, beans and peas. Adjusting the mix can lead to positive shifts in your digestive function, energy levels and even reduce your appetite for carbohydrates or fats which your body may be craving to make up for the unbalanced protein intake.

Whole Grains – What percentage of the carbohydrates that you are ingesting are in the original form that nature put them in? Remember, bread doesn't grow on trees and making fruit juice from fruit would actually burn a significant amount of calories if you didn't have an electric blender! Can you find a way to get more whole grains or whole fruit into your diet?

Reducing Chemical Load – For those that are ready for a bigger shift and have the financial resources to do so, consider gradually increasing the percentage of organic food you are eating each week. If you're on a tighter budget, you can still reduce the chemical load in your body by focusing on adding in non-organic food that is low in chemical content and buying the organic version of only those foods that are most highly toxic. Check the Resources at the end of the book for a list of foods from most to least toxic.

De-Stimulation – If you know that you can't get through a day without your cup (or two or three) of coffee, consider focusing in on gradually reducing the amount and frequency. One easy way to begin is to replace one cup per day with green tea or de-caffeinated coffee. Alternatively, you can have a tall glass of water before brewing up or ordering your next cup to see if it stops you from finishing it.

Personalized Diet – Having been trained at the Institute for Integrative Nutrition®, I'm aware of just how many approaches and schools of thought there are when it comes to the subject of the best way to eat. What I've found to be true is that almost every diet out there works for a certain number of people and also doesn't work for certain number of people. What's important is that you are making educated choices and that you have a clear idea of what actually works for you, in your body, at this time in your life. And then, when it comes to Committed Action mode, as with any other dietary change, it's best to make the changes in stages.

Cleanse/Elimination – And now we have arrived at the inevitable exception to the rule. I've emphasized and re-emphasized the importance of making small changes over time as the best way to go about generating lasting behavioral change. And yet, I have witnessed that cleanses and elimination diets can deliver long term results in shifting eating habits and, even more importantly, clarity about what particular foods are causing particular symptoms in our bodies. Check out the Resources section at the end of the book for a place to start as you educate yourself about this way of jump-starting your time in Committed Action mode for body.

Here are a few more notes to keep in mind as you learn to relate to your body like a well-oiled machine:

○ It's not about which particular exercise(s) you choose it's that you stick with it. As I've said, you can make all the adjustments you see fit to make. Just don't stop, no matter how tempted you are. The fulfillment, power and satisfaction that comes with seeing your plan through to completion is simply invaluable. Whenever you get stuck, I recommend you return to Chapter 9 and re-read it to ensure you are tapping into all the tools available to keep yourself on track.

○ The amount of time it's going to take for you to sustainably shift a behavior pattern is variable depending on the behavior pattern and the current circumstances of your life. While I recommend a minimum of 6 weeks in Committed Action mode, you may find that you'll need to (or want to) continue longer. Once past the six-week mark, trust yourself to know when to "let go of the wheel" and cease the weekly check-in process.

○ It's possible that not all of your habits will stick, especially if you are working all three mini-magnifiers for the body. This is okay as this may simply mean you may have more work to do in Awareness Mode. You can re-approach those that didn't stick the next time you enter Committed Action mode.

○ Finally, don't forget to celebrate your accomplishments! It's critical, especially as you complete your time in Committed Action mode, to find a way to mark the completion and review all you have learned, experienced and accomplished!

Remember, these exercises are my best suggestions for dealing directly with the energetic magnifiers. You are welcome to leverage exercises or modalities that you are already familiar with, search out new ones, or create your own! For the most up-to-date thinking on all of these exercises and to share your experience or get support, you can head to www.consciousliving.ning.com and register for access to the online community.

CHAPTER 11

BECOMING EMOTIONALLY FLUENT

O f the four EMs, the Magnifier of the emotions just may be the one that takes the most courage to engage with deeply. This is because getting in touch with, fully feeling and then sometimes sharing our emotional state with other people requires a willingness to be vulnerable that doesn't always make logical sense at the time. If you then consider that modern society's penchant is to calm every nerve and fix every uncomfortable feeling or bodily symptom with a product, drug or service, you will come to see that engaging with this EM takes courage. It's also ripe for the harvesting and offers us a wealth of gifts.

If you're arriving at this chapter, I'm assuming that you're aware that there are aspects of your personal emotional terrain that are in need of some exploring. I further assume that you're ready to break out the camping gear so you can spend some quality time in the "wild" of the emotions.

But before we set out on the hike, I want to address a bit of a conundrum that we encounter as we engage with the emotions meaningfully. While time spent in Committed Action mode generally requires persistence and rigor, emotions do not lend themselves easily to being pinned down or dealt with on the terms that our minds might want to deal with them. To truly connect with the emotions in real time, one must be willing to have their well laid intentions and plans be interrupted by seemingly irrational and ill-timed intrusions of feeling that may seem to have absolutely no relationship to what's currently going on in your life. It can sometimes seem that emotions are like inconvenient roadblocks on your way to what you "know" is your destination.

So, while this chapter will offer you different exercises that give you access to the realm of emotions, you will need to be willing to be in a dynamic dance with them, sometimes being led on tangents and into dark alleyways and sometimes doing the leading by consciously applying structure to your exploration.

In order to support you in increasing the degree of fluency you have in engaging with your emotions, we're going to re-visit the four core competencies of emotional fluency from Chapter 6.

Thoughts vs. Emotions – Round Two

The first competency to re-visit at a deeper level is the capacity to distinguish thoughts and emotions. In Awareness Mode we discussed how doing this gives you access to more effective communication with those around you. In Committed Action mode, you can begin by first just extending the One Week Satisfaction Booster version of the Thoughts vs. Emotions exercise to two, three or even four weeks. And then, you can begin to take the exercise to the next level by finding opportunities during the day to actually disentangle the thought/emotion collapse in real time (or as close to real time as is feasible).

When you can begin to deal with thought/emotion collapses in real time, you start to get the true power of this exercise. What this requires is your willingness to let go of thoughts that are tied to emotions that are unwanted in favor of different thoughts that generate emotions that are wanted.

So, much like before, you will want to have a place to write down the following each time you are engaging in the exercise:

○ Rate the intensity of the disruption to your daily life on a scale from 1-10, with one being barely noticeable, and ten being nearly paralyzed. The purpose for doing this is so that you can begin to see patterns, over time, that give you clues as to some of the deeper factors driving the disruptions in your daily living.

○ Write down the thoughts that are occurring when you are in this disrupted state. For some people, it's helpful to write more and for others less. You will learn what is right for you. As a guideline, you'd want a minimum of three sentences and a maximum of one page.

○ Now, write down the primary emotion that you are feeling while you are thinking the thoughts you wrote down. You can choose from among the big four (fear, sadness, anger or disgust) **or** describe your emotional state as you see fit. Just be sure that what you are describing is an actual emotion and not more thoughts! An easy way to know that what you are describing is an emotion is if someone could identify the emotion you are feeling simply by looking at you. Another good rule of thumb is that an emotion is generally one word, whereas thoughts can go on and on.

And now, here's where we take it further in Committed Action Mode. Rather than simply getting the thought/emotion collapse and acknowledging it either to yourself or someone else, you are going to come up with an alternate thought about whatever the situation is that is being experienced. You see, much of why we experience unwanted emotions, especially when they recur, is because we are thinking the same thought or thoughts again and again, expecting a different emotional result. So, instead, you will consciously come up with another possible thought about the situation, person or behavior that is associated with this unwanted emotion.

This will likely feel contrived at first. We are so often collapsing thoughts and emotions automatically that we don't actually get to see that it's possible to do any differently. When we increase our emotional fluency and realize that we have a choice in how we direct our mental attention, things get interesting. You see, the thought that you have just collapsed with the emotion is very likely not 100% true. And, even if it IS true, is it worth it to hold onto that thought as true if it causes you unwanted emotion, over and over and over?

So, when you first begin working with this exercise, the idea is to make a small change to the wording of the thought. Let's look at an example. Let's say that you're at the wedding of your cousin with whom you grew up with and with whom you remain very close. When it comes time for the speeches by the best man and maid of honor, you suddenly feel a flash of anger when their college friend stands up to speak. You immediately have the thought "Well, why wasn't I chosen as the best man (or maid of honor)?" "Obviously the groom/bride doesn't value our relationship as much as I do." You can imagine that if you went through the rest of the evening with this thought/emotion combo you would probably not enjoy yourself fully. So, what thought could you come up with instead?

A good example of a small change to the wording of the thought would be something like changing the word "obviously" to "maybe." It may seem simple but changing that word and then actually having that thought/saying it to yourself begins to loosen the grip of the original thought and introduce a different quality to the experience.

As you continue to practice with this exercise, you can begin to go further and get more creative in your thinking. Another thought you could have would be: "I wonder if the reason they didn't choose me to speak is that they would have then had to choose between me and their brother/sister and they just went the easier route for them rather than having to make that kind of choice."

As time goes by and you continue to engage with this exercise, you will find that the need to write things down will lessen. You may find that all you need to do is separate yourself from the situation for a few minutes to get your thoughts in order. And then, eventually, you'll find that you are actually able to complete the whole process in less than a minute, and then less than 30 seconds. Until, eventually, when you have mastered it, you won't even realize you've done the work to switch the thought.

There are two additional exercises you can engage with to further develop your capacity to distinguish thoughts from emotions. The first one is especially great for those who love to be supported by another (a concept we discussed in "What Makes Your Tick – Part Two" in Chapter 9). You can ask someone close to you, who you trust, to assist you in this process. How it works is that you instruct them to listen to you describe a situation where you are having an unwanted emotional experience and then have them ask you questions that are designed to help you to first distinguish your thoughts and emotions and then see the relationship between the two. Some example questions are:

- How did you feel when you thought that?
- Was there any other emotion that was present in that situation?
- Is there another thought you could have had at that moment that would likely have a different emotion associated with it?

Of course, after they have played this role for you, you may find that they ask you to return the favor. And you know what they say about learning: sometimes the best way to learn is to teach!

Finally, as was mentioned earlier in the chapter, working with our emotions doesn't always fit nicely and neatly into a conversation with a friend or a discrete event that comes up during a given day. So, an alternate exercise for those that enjoy a bit more free form expression when they're learning about themselves is to "stream of consciousness" journal about your emotional landscape. What this means is to write without trying to make sense or organize your thoughts. You simply write whatever you are thinking within the broad framework of what happened during the day in your emotional landscape. After getting it all out, you can take a few minutes break (or even sleep on it) and then return to what you've written and see if you can clearly distinguish the emotional content from the thoughts easily or if you now need to distinguish it further.

Owning Your Emotions – Round Deux

I know that it really does seem that someone else is causing you to feel something when you are in the middle of an argument with your lover or a family member who does something that 99.9% of humanity would agree is clearly manipulative and/or evil. Unfortunately, no matter how much it seems like someone else's behavior, words or attitude is generating the emotional response in you, the reality is that your response is yours and yours alone. How do we know this? If you line up five different people and say the exact same sentence to them (a sentence designed to perhaps be mildly insulting, like one insinuating that they don't look very good physically...something on the order of "Did you get enough sleep last night?"), all five people, if asked on a scale of 1-10 how angry they feel, will very likely provide you with a different response.

So then, if you are interested in having power and flexibility in life to be able to roll with the punches and be responsive, rather than reactive to events, people and situations around you, it's in your interests to fully own your own emotions.

Back in Chapter 6, I outlined a 24-hour experiment that is designed to get you present to the different emotions you are feeling, expressing with yourself, and then expressing in the presence of others. In Committed Action mode, you are invited to take on this experiment on a more regular basis. You don't have to spend weeks and weeks monitoring your emotions. However, you can spend multiple afternoons, mornings or evenings per week with it. This regular check in will allow you to have a chance to reflect on your emotional expression when the variety in your life is providing opportunities to connect with and express different (and different levels of intensity) of emotion.

As you begin to build up this emotional record, you can then take a step back and begin to notice what patterns are emerging. There are four major patterns that benefit from closer inspection.

1. Is there one particular emotion that you have a tendency to feel often but not express?

2. Is there an emotion that you are very rarely experiencing?

3. Do you find that there is a particular emotion that you are much more frequently *feeling* in the presence of others and not on your own (or vice-versa)?

4. Is there one emotion that you are very comfortable expressing on your own, but when it comes to *expressing* it to others, you shut down?

The next step is to consider what you are noticing and begin to identify actions. And, the action you take will depend on what you are noticing, so let's take a look at each of these major patterns.

When you notice that there is a particular emotion that you have a tendency to feel often but not express I recommend an exercise that is so simple and completely natural, yet we almost never allow ourselves to do it. All it involves is simply taking some time each day to lay down and feel what you are feeling. There is no particular technique to follow or anything particular to think about. You are simply spending three to five minutes focused on your felt experience rather than your mental one. Consider it an "Emo-Break." Of course, the mind will be present and you will be having thoughts. Your job is to keep bringing your attention to whatever it is you are feeling. You will likely notice that what you're feeling changes during the time you are lying down. The intensity of the emotion will very likely ebb and flow. A good question to start with if you're not sure where to begin is "What is the primary emotion present for me right now?" You can ask the question, allow yourself to feel it fully, and then ask it again and again until the only answer is "ease" or "peace".

If you have any trouble at all with your sleep, I recommend that you do this exercise somewhere other than in your bed so that you can preserve the bedroom for sleeping and sex (not that you can't also do that elsewhere!). ☺ Finally, I also recommend practicing this, at least some of the time, when you are completely alone. In this way, you give yourself maximum space to feel what needs to be felt without having to deal with any explanation afterward if you feel deep anger or sadness and express that vocally.

On the other side of this spectrum, you may come to notice that there is an emotion that you are rarely experiencing. I want to be completely clear that there is absolutely nothing wrong if this is the case. That said, it may be useful for you to set aside some time every few days to check in during this "emo-break" exercise and set the intention of determining if you may be either repressing the emotion you are rarely experiencing or "softening it" by experiencing a less intense version. For example, you may very often experience being frustrated but not let yourself go all the way to anger. Or, you may be okay with feeling listless, but avoid sinking all the way into sadness. We'll take a closer look at this phenomenon a bit later in the chapter when we re-visit the conversation about breadth & depth of emotional experience.

The very same simple exercise can also be employed to help you to connect with feelings that you typically only feel when you are with others and not so much when you are on your own. When you notice this happening regularly, you can set an intention before you lie down to focus a bit more intently on those emotions and see if you can sense for where you might be "tucking" that emotion away from yourself, only to be triggered later when you are with other people.

When you find that you have emotions that you are easily able to feel or express on your own, but aren't able to feel or express in the presence of others, there is a different approach

"We each have a unique learning style. I recommend that, if after a day or two, you are not expanding your level of awareness, you change the exercise that you are engaging with. Please refer to the Resources&References section, under the header for Chapter 5, to learn more about different learning styles."

that must be taken. The first step is to open up some space to feel what you're feeling while in the presence of others. It's important to slowly build up your capacity in this regard. If you like, at first, you can head to the bathroom and utilize the privacy of a stall to give yourself a few minutes to connect with (and maybe type out on your smart phone) your emotional state.

As your capacity to feel emotions that you are not used to feeling around other people expands, you can then begin allowing yourself to actually feel them in real time for a few seconds or longer while in the presence of others. Initially, it's a good idea to allow yourself to feel the emotions but not immediately attach thoughts to them or express them out loud. Then, as you progress further, you can allow your emotional state to fuel your expression.

I know that this can seem scary and even a bit odd at first. You may be asking yourself if it's really worth it to express more of your emotional state in situations where you have habitually suppressed or pushed aside what you are feeling. Much of the reason for our tendency to shy away from emotional expression in a group situation is that most of our experience in this regard is in either witnessing or being on the receiving end of someone else's *projection* of their emotions (fear, anger, jealousy, etc.) on to someone else.

There is a vast difference between projecting your emotions onto someone else and authentically expressing your emotions while at the same time owning them as your own. Let's look at how this looks in your speaking. An example of a projection of your emotions on someone else would sound something like "I wish you would stop making me feel so angry by never putting your dirty clothes in the hamper!" To turn this around and both own *and* authentically express your emotional state would be to say something like "I notice that I feel angry right now and I feel that way when I think about the fact that the dirty clothes are on the floor and not in the hamper." I like to call this process an "emotional re-direct".

It's important to note that the intention here is **not** to edit out the emotional energy that is associated with the situation. The difference is that instead of throwing that energy over to the other person, you feel it for yourself and use language to keep yourself present. It offers you the opportunity to see what's going on for you rather than how the other person is involved. This opens up a space for the other person to witness what's going on for you because they are no longer being judged or projected on to. And once they have the opportunity to witness you, there is a good chance, especially if they care for you, for them to find compassion. They may even look together with you at how to find a solution for the original concern that works for both of you.

When you begin to engage with this exercise you'll realize that there are no shortage of opportunities to practice it. In Committed Action mode, a good place to begin is aiming for an average of one emotional re-direct per day. Sometimes you'll miss a day, so you can aim for seven per week.

I have one final exercise that you can start with, especially if all of this is feeling a bit overwhelming for your day-to-day life. You can begin, perhaps every other day or so, to post a photo or quote that captures your emotional state to your favorite social networking platform. You can even share with people that you are exploring owning your emotions and identifying what you're feeling. In this way you are beginning this process at a safe distance from other people, yet still sharing yourself. This said, I do not recommend that this be the entirely of your focus in Committed Action mode. While identifying and sharing your emotional state is a great jumping off point, the real juice comes when you begin directly strengthening the emotional threads with the people that make up the fabric of your life. We practice identifying and sharing so that we can see ourselves more clearly. This gives us a more complete toolbox for connection with others, as well as ourselves.

Range & Depth

One of the 20th century's most prominent experts on emotion, Robert Plutchik, created a complex and integrative emotional model that both expands the palette of emotion beyond the primary emotions of anger, joy, fear and sadness and also offers a perspective on the varying degrees of depth at which one can experience emotions. To support you in expanding both the range and depth of your emotional experience, we'll leverage his model to guide your exploration.

What's required is to sensitize yourself further than you did in Awareness Mode so that you are not only aware of **what** you are feeling but also the intensity of that feeling. For example, there is an anger spectrum that increases in intensity from mere annoyance, up through anger and eventually to rage. Similarly, when it comes to happiness, you can simply be at peace/feeling serene, you might be joyful or you could be all the way through the roof into ecstasy.

In addition to depth, there is also a very broad range of emotional expression. Plutchik described additional emotions beyond the four that we began exploring back in Awareness Mode. A list of these emotions, which you can use for the next exercise, can be found in the Resources section of the book.

To set the stage for a deeper exploration of your emotional range and depth, the first step is to connect with and stimulate the broader range of emotions available. One way to go about this is to create a picture album, either virtual or physical. The idea is to take some time to gather images that evoke different emotional responses in you. After referencing the list of emotions at the back of the book, you can either use magazines as a source for photos or just type the emotion into your favorite search engine and choose from the images displayed. You can then download the images and create a folder for each emotion on your computer. I recommend a minimum of 3 photos for each emotion. This simple act of curating your own personal "emotion museum" will, in and of itself, very likely have you more sensitive to your emotional landscape throughout the day.

If you respond more intensely to video, you can create a similar kind of album utilizing clips from the Internet that evoke the different emotions. Once you've created the photo album or video vault, you can check in with it daily to help you uncover what emotions may be lurking underneath the surface for you.

Then, to take things a step further, you can start adding an intensity level to the Emotional Tracker from Chapter 6. You can use a scale from 1-10. So, for example, if you're feeling just slightly annoyed, you can rate yourself a 1 or a 2 and if you're seething mad, you can rate yourself a 9 or a 10. Again, I refer you to the Resources chapter for more details on the emotional spectrums. By applying your attention in this way you will be able to see if, over time, you tend to only experience certain emotions mildly and very rarely intensely. As you begin to see this, you can go into your emo-breaks with the intention to explore greater depth of feeling and expression for those emotions. I invite you to bring a sense of play and fun to this endeavor as thoughts of resistance can easily sabotage your exploration and block you from experiencing the gift of energy that feeling your emotions *fully* provides.

One final option for evoking deeper emotional response, though a bit more cumbersome to execute, may appeal to you. If you live in or near a city, you can scan the reviews and descriptions for whatever plays, operas or dance performances are currently on and then get yourself some tickets. If you do take on this option, I recommend bringing a note pad with you so that you can note anything that comes up for you while the performance is happening (or during the intermission).

Consciously exploring, evoking and expressing your emotions on a more regular basis in this way is one of the most potent ways to engage with the Energy Magnifier of the emotions. The principle behind this reality is that the energy that is required to keep your emotions bottled up and unexpressed is freed up when you increase your capacity to feel your emotions fully and especially when you can begin allowing yourself to feel them in the moment they come up. This leads us to the final core competency for emotional fluency.

Taking Action (In The Moment & After the Fact)

As your level of emotional fluency increases, what you'll begin to notice next is that there are times when it's appropriate for you to share what you're seeing with those you care most about or have a relationship with, the health of which is critical to your overall life satisfaction. Back in Awareness Mode there was an exercise, which alluded to this, and here in Committed Action Mode, it's time to take it up a notch.

What you're now interested in determining is what are the appropriate actions to take in response to the emotion you're feeling relative to another person or a situation. And there are two pieces to this. Initially, it's about taking a look back at a situation where you were experiencing relatively intense emotion and then "returning to the scene of the crime" to see what could have gone differently.

For example, if you notice that you are regularly experiencing the emotion of anger and/or frustration when you are sitting in the daily briefing meeting at work, you could take a few minutes after the meeting ends to see if there is a conversation you can have with a colleague or your boss so that something changes in the way the meeting is run. Or perhaps there is a new way that you can set up your workday or week that would allow to have some pre-meeting conversations that would have things go differently during the meeting itself. There are very few unworkable situations that do not respond to either a sincere conversation, some new action on your part or a restructuring of how you are relating to what's going on around you.

The same thing goes for other experiences, such as a recurring sadness with your partner or persistent fear around your health. If you are super clear on what you are feeling, often the key to the shift you're looking for lies in the doing. So, if this is you, practice getting clear at the end of the day about the unwanted emotion you felt the strongest or deepest that day and then get clear on what needs to happen tomorrow so that this emotional energy isn't wasted. You can schedule some new action in your calendar or send an email to initiate a conversation with the person you sense would make the most sense to talk to about it.

If you're wondering how to best set yourself up for a positive and effective outcome if what seems necessary is a conversation, a quick review of the Thought vs. Emotion section of this chapter is in order.

And then there is the process of shifting towards taking action in real time, when you are noticing that emotions are bubbling to the surface in relationship with other people. A good place to start is to just begin peppering your conversations with the question, "I was just wondering, what do you feel about this situation?" Or, "How do you feel about the quality of our relationship right now?" While some people may not be comfortable answering, the mere fact of asking the question opens up a new dimension in your relationship. Once the question is out there, it shows the other person that you are interested in more than just a particular outcome. Instead, the other person can now get (even if only on a sub-conscious level) that you are interested in their emotional experience as well. This creates a level of intimacy that did not exist before and very often creates new possibilities of relating that did not exist prior.

And, even if the person you are interacting with is not

comfortable or ready to share their emotional state, what you have done is open up the chance for them to ask you for yours or even for you to simply share yours.

Remember, these exercises are my best suggestions for dealing directly with the energetic magnifiers. You are welcome to leverage exercises or modalities that you are already familiar with, search out new ones, or create your own! For the most up-to-date thinking on all of these exercises and to share your experience or get support, you can head to www.consciousliving.ning.com to register for access to the online community.

Something important to remember as you begin to weave emotional questions and sharing into your conversations is that we all have a strong tendency, as discussed previously, to collapse emotions and thoughts. And this is okay. It's simply important to be aware of this so that you can catch yourself doing it and also, over time, ask deeper follow-up questions that invite those around you to share more of themselves and to be clear (and help them be clear) about the difference between their thoughts and emotions.

It's how you respond to those emotional states that will determine the speed with which you make the changes in your life necessary to realize your full potential.

It's also important when you move from Awareness Mode, (where most of your effort is self-focused), to Committed Action mode, (where you are more regularly interacting with others), that you take care to tread carefully and gently in your dealings and communication. And, even still, you might occasionally rub others in a way that they don't like. This is okay, as long as you are willing to take full responsibility for the fact that you have involved them in your personal growth journey and that you communicate that you are still learning how to be the best human being you can be.

And remember, not every emotion you are feeling is actually meant to be communicated. So, discern for yourself if the expression of that emotion in important to your growth or to your aim of living an empowered, satisfied life before you share it with others. Sometimes, the emotion is there simply to light the way to a new way of thinking or acting that has everything to do with you and does not require your sharing this shift with others.

You may have noticed, especially if you have also read the Committed Action chapter on Body, that I have not included a specific and structured action plan sheet for you to use. This is intentional as working with the emotions is inherently susceptible to frequent and sometimes extended detours. So, rather than creating a structured plan at the beginning to keep you on track, I recommend that you set aside some review time 1, 2 or 3 times per week (you'll learn what works for you) as you begin. You may find as your tour of Committed Action mode in the emotions continues onward, that a more structured approach works for you. If this is the case, you can create a sheet similar to the one we used in the previous chapter for body but use the four competencies to organize your weekly actions.

Finally, remember that we are not working with and focusing on the emotions with the intention of subduing them or getting rid of them. So, if you go into Committed Action mode with the intention of "dealing with" or "trying to get a handle on" your emotions, you will be disappointed. Instead, we are interested in leveraging and tuning in to your emotional state. We are valuing the information, wisdom and direction that our emotional state can offer us. Throughout life, you will continue to feel anger, joy, fear and sadness to varying degrees. It's how you respond to those emotional states that will determine the speed with which you make the changes in your life necessary to realize your full potential.

CHAPTER 12

MENTAL GYMNASTICS

We're racing down the northeast coast of Spain, intermittently going in and out of tunnels with flashes of the deep blue Mediterranean in between. The train is carrying weekend escapees of the city of Barcelona. The sounds of the Spanish language are everywhere.

It's the day after I've been released from the hospital after having a stroke. I'm in surprisingly good shape, physically. I've got energy and am excited to be alive. I guess it makes sense, given I had been lying down for five days in a hospital bed. Still, a stranger would never have guessed I had experienced a stroke a week prior.

My mother, sister, and I are on our way to the beach town of Sitges in Catalunya, Spain. They had flown in a few days earlier to support me after the stroke, and we were on our way to spend a relaxing day on the beach together. The train is full and most people are busy staring out the window or on their mobile devices.

But not us! My sister and I are having an intense conversation about my strong desire to be on a boat with my friends the next afternoon. She is incredulous that I would even consider such a thing while she and Mom are in town. Emotions are running high and we're duking it out verbally, occasionally raising our voices and gesticulating, eye rolling or sighing forcefully and neither of us feel satisfied (and let's not forget my Mother, who is witnessing two of her children in a verbal boxing match, in public, one day after I've left the hospital). Now, the thing you need to know about my sister is that she is a formidable force to be reckoned with. I love her very much. And while we are so very alike in many ways, we can also be intensely at odds at times.

As I felt my level of satisfaction sinking, I remember two concepts (thoughts vs. perspectives and simultaneous broadcasting vs. true communication, both from Chapter 7) and bring these concepts into my active awareness. I was able to see that some of what was going on was that my sister and I had different concepts for what proper behavior is when family, who live halfway across the world, are visiting. So we could shift the conversation to looking at that, instead of dwelling only in the emotional content or in the particulars of the boat party.

The situation required all the energy I could muster from the EM of Mind while also keeping myself open to the messages from all of the other EMs. If you want to be able to have power, and generate satisfaction, even when in the kind of situation such as the one described here, you`re ready to move into Committed Action Mode for the EM of mind.

As I checked in with my non-verbal communication and noticed I was standing over my sister in a way that might communicate that I wanted to control or dominate the situation, I modified my position, occasionally, to squat and be with her eye to eye, sensitized to how she may be experiencing the EM of Body. I incorporated some speaking that referenced my emotional experience and what I imagine her emotional experience might be. I also acknowledged our soul connection in this lifetime and how I see that as unbreakable, helping us both to tap into the EM of Self.

Now, get this. The next day, I realized that the boat trip was not until the following Sunday anyway. So, the whole exchange hadn't even needed to happen, or hadn't it? Our bond is stronger than ever as I assist her in planning her wedding here in Spain. ☺

While Chapter 7 introduced and prepared you for practicing the individual steps to a complex and intricate dance, this chapter is about beginning to bring all the steps together and dance as if everyone is watching. You will develop your capacity to be responsive rather than reactive in your thinking. Here, while you stay in the mind, you will also create a sufficiently different (actually, broader) perspective to re-frame or re-contextualize with.

In order to set the stage for this dance performance, let's revisit the four main distinctions of the first chapter on mind and infuse them with a new level of clarity and power.

Let's start by combining two concepts: 1) most of your thoughts are borrowed and 2) there are thoughts and then there are perspectives or worldviews. Instead of resisting this reality, what if, since it's practically inevitable that you're going to borrow them anyway, you were to purposefully borrow some thoughts and/or worldviews from people who have achieved a state of being that you aspire to? How carefully are you paying attention to the ideas and people you are surrounded by? Each person around you influences you in some way, no matter how clear you are about who you already are.

We are all sponges for information and ideas. While you don't really have too much control over whether you are a sponge, you do have choice with which «channel» or channels you are tuned in to, whether electronic or in human form (friends, family, etc.), and therefore the quality and/or type of the "informational liquid" you are soaking up.

One of the great things about living in the Information Age is that you most likely have access to the Internet. And so, you can benefit from the wealth of historically realized and practiced perspectives and thought forms that it chronicles. These include the most influential and wise human beings that have ever lived (both dead and still living).

Your greatest challenge is not access to different thinking, but instead being able to focus on the appropriate thoughts or perspectives for you, at this time, and *then, equally importantly,* not getting attached to one particular thought form for longer than is beneficial. This is not to say that you are meant to be shifting what thoughts or world-views you identify with at the whims of your fleeting desires and ever-changing emotions. More on this in a bit. However, if a thought or worldview is consistently and repeatedly generating an experience of life that is not satisfying, it's time to change things up, yes? You see, you are a unique, individual creation and there may not be one worldview that is appropriate for you over the course of your entire lifetime.

In the Resources section at the end of the book, I provide a starter list of historical wisdom leaders, which I have created based on my own personal journey in this lifetime. Please feel free to check out my list and see who resonates with you in an authentic way. As you begin to delve into their perspective, you can actually, over time, begin to think "as them," and you can then ask yourself the question, at times, "What would (insert name of historical wise person here) think/say/do in this situation?"

Next, let's revisit the idea of empowered vs. disempowered thinking. When you become a master of empowerment, you will regularly and spontaneously ask yourself questions that give you access to a shift from "dis" to "em" powered. Questions like:

> "What might be the greater purpose for this situation/ relationship/challenge?"
> "What might my future self tell me about this way of thinking?"
> "How might this challenging situation lead to something great later on?"

If you spend a little bit of time, you will arrive at a personalized question or group of questions that is particularly effective for you in revving up the level of empowerment in your thinking.

Equally important as asking new, empowering questions is to simultaneously not resist (and, in fact, accept) the emotions you were, or are currently, feeling as a result of the disempowered thinking. It's important that when you ask new questions, that you're doing it freely and not in order to fix or avoid an emotion that you were not previously allowing yourself to feel. Don't skip the feeling of the emotion in your rush to empower yourself with new thoughts and perspectives and miss the full experience. When you allow yourself to first feel the emotion that was the initial indication of a need for change, you expand your capacity to be compassionate with yourself, and thus with others. Being in a state of compassion more often is one of the primary ways to expand your level of satisfaction in life.

In the clarity that exists after a full feeling of an emotion, new actions often become obvious and compelling. And, if not action, then some new way of viewing a situation you are in will enter your state of mind. In this way, you allow the energy you just accessed in the EM of emotion to spill over into the EM of the mind. This is something that must be experienced and can not simply be understood by the mind alone. It's rare that more than two or three days go by when I don't engage this process. I typically utilize Somato Respiratory Integration.

Back in Chapter 7, we briefly touched on the concept of Simultaneous Broadcasting vs. True Communication. Now that you are in Committed Action mode, let's go further. Beyond the basic techniques of ensuring you are actually communicating with someone else, which we touched on in Chapter 7, there are some powerful ways to get into new depths of communication with those you care most about (and sometimes even those you've just met). There are four particularly powerful ways to shift from simultaneous broadcasting to true communication.

The first is to use what I call the soul filter during your conversations and in your relationships. This is no small feat! In practical terms, you want to listen to everything someone is saying as if it were their highest self speaking directly to you. This may be an appropriate time to review Chapter 8, especially if you tend to have a weak connection to the EM of Self. The fastest way I know how to put on the soul filter is to assume that, in every moment, the universe/God/our highest self is trying to communicate with us. And not only is the universe/God/our highest self trying to communicate, but they actually want to give us the key to experiencing satisfaction in that very moment. If you come from that place and understand that sometimes your soul is speaking to you through another, you will listen to people for the gold that they are speaking to you. You don't even need to believe that this is true to reap the benefits from this way of listening. You see, just in choosing to listen in this way, you will be far more present than usual and so the entire experience of communicating with someone will satisfy you in new ways.

I like to put on the soul filter often when I'm speaking with those whom I know love me. I recommend you start with those kinds of people before putting it on with others as having this filter on opens you up and has you vulnerable in ways that, perhaps, you typically aren't. And so, often when someone I love and whom I know loves me says something that could be interpreted as negative or judgmental, I will put on the soul filter and see if there could be any truth in what they've said. And sometimes, while there may not have been something truthful in what they said directly, if I look and follow where I imagine they were going in saying what they said, I find something of value for me.

The second is to broaden your attention to the non-verbal aspects of communication. Because communicating with others is a daily occurrence and it's while we're communicating with others when the mind is typically most highly engaged (our ego is at great risk when talking with others, so the mind goes on high alert), this is a powerful leverage point for sustained shifts in the way you access the EM of the mind. This means not only picking up the non-verbal cues of the person you are communicating with but also utilizing non-verbal communication yourself.

A great place to begin opening your mind to this kind of communication is with the book *The 5 Love Languages*. While the book itself is about how to love another person effectively, the concept of the love languages is a great way to blow the roof off of what you are habitually focused on when communicating (that is: simply what's being said and maybe what's not being said). You will be introduced to the idea of physical touch as one of the modes of communication. I personally find that physical touch is an important way to interrupt the otherwise non-stop nature of mental/verbal communication. You may find this to be the case for you, or you may want to explore the many other modes of non-verbal communication. I have included a link in the Resources section at the end of the book (the one and only link to Wikipedia that I have included in this book).

How this can look in day-to-day communication, is in testing and consciously altering the amount of distance between yourself and the person you are talking with (this includes leaning in to the camera in a video conversation). It can also include occasionally touching the other person you are talking with (of course, in a non-sexual way, unless your intention is to be sexual and that is appropriate with that person and in that context, for your culture).

Some other examples are pausing and looking into the other person's eyes or bringing attention to whether you or they are crossing arms across chest or slouching in some way. To begin to learn more about the significance of each of these non-verbal communications, I refer again to the Wikipedia article referenced in the previous paragraph.

Third, is to consciously bring both gratitude *and* acknowledgement into communication with others and even with yourself. These are each, on their own, powerful and probably deserving of an entire book themselves. In a way, acknowledgement is actually a specialized version of gratitude in that it's gratitude for a person's existence in your life or something particular that they represent for you and that you then communicate to them about. You can also acknowledge someone for a particular action they took that impacted you positively.

Ask yourself how often you are currently taking the time to acknowledge the people in your life that you are grateful for. For some people, it's easier to begin the practice of gratitude by expressing it via acknowledgement to the people around them, rather than looking at what they are grateful for about their own life. Whichever way works for you, what's important is that you give some airtime to what it is that brings you joy and is already working well at this very moment. Some can confuse this with "ass kissing." The difference here is in the background intention. Acknowledgement is an action taken freely and with no expectation of a particular response or reciprocal action. It's a gift, both for the person being acknowledged and the one doing the acknowledging.

And, finally, you can begin navigating the choppy waters of respecting others' preferences and ways of communicating *while still being yourself in communication.* Look for common ground in communication with others. Here, you're generating a unique and ever evolving set of agreements with those who are up for that level of communication and relatedness with you. It requires that you know your style of communication and have sufficient awareness of the "why" behind whatever it is you are saying. More on this in just a bit.

There is a myth that agreement is the preferred state of being in relationship. I just said, in the previous paragraph, that finding common ground is important. And this is true, however, while common ground is important, it does not imply that we are striving for sameness. Wouldn't it be so uninteresting, if your communication style was exactly the same as the communication styles of all those you loved? Instead of insisting on similar communication styles with those around you, work toward agreement on some rules of engagement *rather than agreement on thinking.* Here are some examples of some rules I've used in the past:

○ Avoid the use of the words "always" and "never".
○ Be willing to modulate the tone of your voice (another way to say this is to be responsible for any emotional content that may be infusing your words).
○ Spend some time communicating both compassionately and non-verbally (remember this from earlier in the chapter?). This can look like eye gazing or simply maintaining some kind of physical contact while speaking with someone in situations where communication is breaking down.

When you create rules, you will break them. The critical thing is to empower those around you to point out when this happens and then to remember that you empowered them to do that for the very reason that sometimes you will slip. *And, don't forget compassion for yourself.*

In reality, not everyone around you will be up for this level of intensity or depth of communication. And that's okay because it's actually not necessary to have this level of conversation with everyone around you at all times. While not everyone will be up for it, if it's important to you, you'll find people who are.

You can start by identifying what your needs/preferences are in communication and also what you want to create/generate/experience as a result of your communications. What needs are you intending to meet through communication?

Consider that there are many possible reasons that human beings communicate. Sometimes we are communicating simply to deal with something logistical (when/where/what/who) and sometimes we want to be seen/gotten/understood. Other times, it's simply to experience or share love or compassion. These are just three possible reasons, and you can probably imagine others. And so, each time you begin a conversation, if you can be aware of what you and/or the other person is looking for in the conversation, you are setting yourself up for a fruitful and satisfying interchange.

One way you can make it feel more real is to take a pause during a conversation with someone and ask them what they most want to experience as a result of the conversation. Another way to ask this is, "What is your intention in this conversation?" You can reference the intentions in the previous paragraph and also explore other ones you may have. Alternatively, you can excuse yourself and head outside for some fresh air or to the bathroom and ask yourself the same questions. The interesting thing is that the different people in a conversation can have different intentions and they can all be met. It requires both awareness and willingness on the part of all people involved.

To operate at this level you need to have spent a fair bit of time in Awareness Mode to be able to **both** assess what is motivating your communication in any given moment **and** lead a conversation with others who may be less aware of what is motivating their communication in the moment.

Oh, and one last thing. If you think you're going to achieve fundamental changes in your way of thinking by tapping in to only the EM of the mind (i.e. with better/improved or more evolved thinking) alone, you are in for a rude awakening. One of the most important aspects of successfully being in Committed Action mode for the Mind, is being able to "roll with the punches" to incorporate the energy from other EM's while you are refining your thinking. When it comes to Committed Action mode in the EM of the Mind, the other EMs will make themselves known as well. And, it's your job to welcome that input in as you take new actions, create new ways of thinking, and re-organize your life for your next phase of development.

Now, it's time to take some of the exercises from the initial chapter on the EM of the Mind and go deeper with them. In addition, there are some new exercises to consider as you take yourself into this mode of actively engaging with your thoughts and perspectives. Let's dive in!

One of the keys to Committed Action mode is the "wax on, wax off" nature of the way you are engaging with your life. In other words, it's important that there is some degree of regularity when engaging with the exercises I'm about to outline for you. So, as soon as you settle on the exercise or exercises that you are going to engage with, the very next step is to determine whether you want to "go it alone" or get supported by a coach or someone else clearly committed to both your development and the shift you want to see in your life. Some of the exercises, in fact, require another person to engage with properly. Others, while you could work them alone, you may find you would benefit from working with them along with someone else.

Exposing The Monologue (In Committed Action Mode)

First, take a moment to return to Chapter 7 to review the first part of this exercise.

The second piece of the exercise is to then take a few moments to review what you wrote and circle the sentence or phrase that is actionable. By actionable, I mean you are looking for the thought or phrase that points to an obvious action you can take to increase your level of satisfaction in the coming day. Or, find a sentence or phrase that is particularly disempowering which you would clearly benefit from dealing with head-on.

Finally, take an action in the coming day that you weren't already going to take as a result of what you saw. For example, if one of the thoughts you wrote down was "I'm really tired and it's hard for me to focus right now," you might consider re-organizing your evening calendar for the coming day to allow for the space to get to bed earlier. Or, if one of the thoughts is, "I don't understand why my partner was in such a bad mood last night," you could send them a text or ask them if there's anything on their mind that they'd like to share with you or if there's anything you can support them with during the coming day.

This exercise is a simple, but very direct, way of beginning to interact with your thoughts in a way that is something other than passive. While it takes time to master the art of

"We each have a unique learning style. I recommend that, if after a day or two, you are not expanding your level of awareness, you change the exercise that you are engaging with. Please refer to the Resources&References section, under the header for Chapter 5, to learn more about different learning styles."

interacting with them in a way that leaves you fully empowered, the simple act of exposing them begins to shift what's possible for you in your life.

Your Customized Personal Mantra (In Committed Action Mode)

Again, first, take a moment to return to Chapter 7 to review the first part of this exercise.

When you have settled on the full sentence, practice saying it to yourself non-stop for two minutes, two or three times per week. For the first few times, you may find that you need to read it to yourself. Ideally, you want to get to the point where you don't need to read it and you can, instead, generate it naturally, yourself.

You may find that, after you have practiced this exercise a few times that you come to a place where you can create a more generalized phrase that can be effective for shifting your mental state no matter what particular disempowered thought you may be having. If this occurs, congratulations, you have just created your own personal mantra! ☺

Scheduling Empowered Thinking (After Mining Your Thoughts)

Here as well, take a moment to return to Chapter 7 to review the first part of this exercise.

As discussed, while you may not strike gold on the first try, I encourage you to keep digging! While gold may elude you at first, you will turn up something interesting that will leave you in a more empowered mental state moving forward.

Lastly, if you don't typically take action solely based on new insight, be sure to schedule whatever action you have seen to take into your calendar.

There is a way to take this exercise to the next level when you're ready to, "take the bull by the horns." You can watch a video, listen to an audio recording or read a chapter in a book each morning for 5 days that relates to the area of life that is suffering from the greatest amount of disempowered thinking. Then, put something in your calendar, that is a result of what you learned for that same day. The cumulative effect of doing this every day for five days is significantly more powerful than simply occasionally doing it. You may need a buddy to develop the discipline required to stick to it for five days in a row.

Mind Cleansing Buddy

This is a powerful technique that I employ regularly with my coaching clients to help them see themselves more clearly. You can practice this with the same person each time, or spread the wealth amongst multiple people in your circle.

Speak your thoughts aloud and have the other person repeat them back to you, the way they heard them (you instruct them to repeat back what you said as closely as possible to what you actually said). I recommend you go one sentence at a time. The final piece is to, when finished, share what has shifted for you as a result of hearing your own thoughts reflected back to you from another person. You can also ask the other person if they see any new actions you could take in response to the thinking, especially if that thinking is disempowered in some way.

The power of this exercise lies in your vulnerability and that you are inserting gaps and pauses in your thinking which allows fresh sprouts of new and different thoughts to emerge from the manure/ detritus of whatever putrid thinking is inhabiting your mind.

Has The Snake Outgrown Its Skin?

This exercise is called for when you are aware of a grouping of disempowered thoughts that have some relationship to each other and that seem to persist, no matter how much work you've done in Awareness Mode with them. The next step is to spend some time, stepping back to distinguish what belief or worldview gives power to the disempowered thoughts.

You can ask questions like: "Who did I learn these thoughts from and how did *they* see the world?" or "Are there other thoughts that I could have or that others might think when in the same set of circumstances?" You can do this work with someone if you get stopped working with it on your own. Another way to take the exercise further is to have a conversation with the person that you borrowed the thoughts from and ask them to help you find another worldview that would leave you more empowered.

It Takes A Village

Here, you create a group. The group can take whatever form works for you and the others in the group (some options include: via email list, Facebook, conference call, video call, or even in-person meet ups). I recommend starting out with no more than five people. The idea it to create an intentional community around some common interest related to empowered thinking. One way this could work is that group members post thoughts that are troubling, bothering or disempowering them. And then, the rule is that the only comments on the thought are:

1. questions from the other participants (no coaching/answers)
2. a revision of the original thought from the original post-er or a response to a question
3. gratitude/acknowledgement

This can work better for some people with a group of strangers, and for others amongst a group of close friends.

Another option is to commit to each other to share one empowered thought, per person, per day. Or, you can come up with whatever frequency works for each individual or the group. And then the rule is that any comment on the thought has to be positive/supportive and involve either:

1. acknowledgment of how that thought is true about the one who initially offered the thought, in the eyes of the commenter, or
2. a reflection on how the thought can be true/relates to the one now commenting

As with all of the exercises in committed action mode, it's the repetition and regularity that really begins to re-wire the way you think.

Practicing Having Fun With Your Thoughts

Here, you begin to see just how pointless it is to identify fully with any one thought or one way of seeing things that have occurred in the past. You begin to become acquainted with the malleability of our perceived reality.

There are two fun and powerful ways to practice:

1. Identify a thought that you entertain regularly which disempowers you. Next, create a thought that completely contradicts the original one. Finally, and this is the kicker, identify the area of your life in which the original thought is actually useful or appropriate and in which area of life the second one works. Laughter is good medicine during this exercise, especially if you begin getting too serious.

2. Write down a painful story from your past, in the form you currently have it in. Then, take out a fresh sheet of paper and write the very same story from another person's perspective, who is somehow empowered by what happened in the story. Make it so completely different than the way you currently tell it, that it strains credulity. What's more ridiculous, doing this exercise or maintaining the disempowering story for as long as you have?

Rapid Fire Mini Meditations

Here again, we start with a disempowered thought and then set a timer to meditate for 1 or 2 minutes. Then, either write down what you saw in meditation about that thought or return to the thought and see what you can now write newly about the situation and/or the thought. You can do this as many times as you like, and I recommend a minimum of three cycles. The meditation can be of whichever type you fancy, the key is in the observing of your thinking.

Tapping Into Non-Linear Thinking

With this exercise, you can break the shackles of linear thinking to dip more deeply into the infinite well of creation from which all thinking emanates. Here, instead of focusing on any disempowered thinking, you'll be peering into the as-yet formless future reality that you are moving toward.

There are two different approaches to choose from here. The first is inspired by an experience I had with Raven Dana of Stress Wizard Coaching. You can begin by setting a timer for three minutes and then allow your mind to wander down the path into your future. Allow all of your senses (sight, sound, smell, touch and taste) to be stimulated by what's coming. Engage your brain in this sensory experience that is not very different from dreaming. After the alarm goes off, promptly write down those elements that stuck out from the experience. If you are so inspired, continue writing and see what else shows up. Allow yourself to "not make sense" in your writing...after all, you are dreaming up a future here...it probably won't make sense if it's solely based on what you've already experienced or already know. Finally, allow yourself to put into words, spoken aloud, what you experienced. Feel free to speak new things that were not there for you in the first two parts of the exercise.

Another approach is to begin leafing through magazines or Google Image search for visual elements that somehow (and it doesn't have to make logical sense) evoke a sense of a future reality. You can then put together a collage of these images in the way that feels best to you. You can even create multiple collages, one for the past reality of your life, or a particular area of life, one for the present, and finally one for the future. Finally, note the similarities AND differences between the past, current and future realities.

You can do either of these two exercises as many times as you want. The well never runs dry.

Soul Brother/Sister

Here you choose to empower one person with whom you will be agreeing to listen to (and vice-versa) with the soul filter we discussed earlier in this chapter. The intention: to support each other in learning to hear your soul voices. You can create a list of questions that shine light on the current perspectives in areas of your lives and ask these questions to each other a minimum of once per week. These questions can have the flavor of what a wise soul would ask a suffering mind. For example: "How could what is currently happening in your life be for your greatest long term good?" or "If everything in creation were perfect in this moment, what is perfect about the situation you find yourself in?" or "Where can love be more fully expressed in this area of your life?" Feel free to imagine your own questions, so long as they tap into the perfection of all that is.

Remember, these exercises are my best suggestions for dealing directly with the energetic magnifiers. You are welcome to leverage exercises or modalities that you are already familiar with, search out new ones, or create your own! For the most up-to-date thinking on all of these exercises and to share your experience or get support, you can head over to www.consciousliving.ning.com to register for access to the online community.

CHAPTER 13

PRACTICING GRACE

So, you say you want a revolution (in the way you experience living)? Well, it's gonna take your focused attention, some discipline *and* a willingness to have periods of your life go "off script." And yet, when you look back, before you leave the planet, you'll recognize those times as the ones when your Self triumphed over You; when the fear melted away for a moment to allow for some magic to happen through you.

It may seem odd to you that you would have done so much work with the mind, emotions and body, building and crafting your personalized, satisfied life, only to seemingly give all that up to go "off script" and dwell in the EM of Self, during which time you may or may not maintain the same kind of relationship with the other EM's. And yet, you'll know it's time to engage in Committed Action mode with the Self when you have developed a connection with the other EM's that is both strong enough and flexible enough to support you in fully engaging with your Self, at least for a period of time.

What do I mean by going "off-script"? Well, as you'll learn when you move into Committed Action mode around Self, there are divine forces that are influencing your life experience and they *can be* powerful and disruptive to any attachments you may have.

That said, there is one super compelling reason to engage in Committed Action mode (when the time is right), with its attendant disruption and it is this: you will deepen your trust in yourself/ others/the universe. This may sound like a small thing, but it is not. When you develop this trust, you are strengthened and emboldened to be yourself, make decisions and create whole new futures for yourself that are wildly and deeply fulfilling.

There are two sides of the coin when it comes to engaging with this EM. Both sides of the coin are a gift, and both sides contain gifts for both you and those you influence.

The first side is that you will get in touch with exactly what you are uniquely designed to bring to or express in the world. The full expression of this is inherently a gift to others, whether it finds expression in your profession or not.

The second side is that you will now be subject to forces that may throw you off balance from time to time and can cause temporary unpleasantness. The gift for you is that you now get to reorganize into the next greatest version of yourself. And then, the gift for others is that when you go off balance, you provide others the opportunity to give their gifts to you.

Are You Letting Go or Are You Reaching For Life?

One of the most influential mentors I've so far had in this lifetime is a man named Donald Epstein. He is a master at delivering wisdom and is courageous in being willing to express that wisdom in a way that challenges some of the tenets of "counter-cultural" or New Age thinking.

It was in his presence when I first understood that all of the focus on "letting go" of things can be a hindrance to actually living.

What I've noticed in my own life is that when I get clear about the future my Self is here to experience, and then begin taking action toward it, I very naturally and easily let go of anything that doesn't match that future. Or, even if not naturally and easily, I find a way, because the future vision is even more of the experience I want than the one I am currently having. Part of this involves surrendering control and part of it is being very clear about what I want.

So, if you find yourself focusing or obsessing on what you need to "let go of," perhaps it's time to shift your focus to what your Self is calling you toward. And, you may not know yet exactly what that is. Later in the chapter, you'll be exposed to some exercises that will help this process along.

Also later in the chapter, I'll talk about an important pitfall to be aware of when engaging in Committed Action mode with the EM of

Self. So, be sure to keep reading for that one.

Let's take a look at an important knowing that you may have begun to realize about your Self in Awareness Mode that you'll now want to consider more closely as you engage in Committed Action mode for the EM of Self. Where are you along the sliding scale of historical archetypes for the self-realized? Hermit on the mountaintop on one side to ashram participant or leader on the other.

In other words, do you connect with your Self with greater intensity and clarity when you focus on you or when you are out there with others? Or, perhaps you are somewhere in the middle?

Let's take a closer look at the two extremes first, before we go any further.

The Community of Selves

One way that human beings have been enjoying connecting with their Selves for millennia is to gather in groups in some kind of organized fashion to explore the "big questions." This has taken many different forms from Socrates and his students in Athens engaged with the Socratic Method (a series of questions designed to help individuals understand their underlying beliefs) to the preachers in churches, rabbis in temples and mullahs/imams in mosques all over the world. For thousands of years, these have been places where people of faith can gather to explore and attempt to make real for themselves in their own lives the teachings of those long gone from the land of the living in the ancient wisdom traditions of Christianity, Judaism, and Islam.

That said, a myriad of paths exist to help access the Self. For some, being a member of a yoga studio and engaging with that community is what's needed to assist them in plugging in to the EM of Self.

In fact, it's been my experience that any grouping of people who are out to support one another's growth and development as human beings can provide access to the EM of Self.

For example, I have started a Project Laboratory in my apartment where people who have projects they have been procrastinating about and who normally labor alone come, once a week, to share a space and to support and encourage one another to complete those projects. On one level, this is a practical way to generate accountability and momentum, and at the level of Self, I know that I'm giving my gift of assisting others in living their best lives while receiving the gift of community and the knowing that what I'm doing in hosting the Laboratory makes a difference, not only for the people attending, but for all the people that those projects will ultimately impact.

You could create something similar or something different. The key elements are that there are more than 3 people and that there is some stated intention that is beyond simply the material world. The group has to be impacting the participants at the level of Self, meaning that somehow it shifts their way of being (for example from being a procrastinator to being a person of action). Or, if you'd prefer, you can look around for existing opportunities of this type (meetup.com might be a good place to start).

The One Self

Since at least the time of the Buddha, and very likely since even earlier times, some have gone inward to access the Self. Meditation and mindfulness practices are the most well known forms of this kind of connection to Self. Self-applied Somato Respiratory Integration, which has been referenced frequently in this book, is another tool for this kind of connection. A self-generated yoga practice is another example.

Being in nature is another way to deepen your connection with Self on your own. For some, taking a certain amount of time per day, week, month, or year to be only with themselves, in a remote place that relieves them of the usual social, work, and day-to-day responsibilities or activities is how they best maintain or develop their connection to the EM of Self.

If you're on this end of the spectrum, it may be about designing your own personal Self-access regime. It may take some time to work out. You'll get your starter kit later in this chapter.

Balancing The Two

The thing is, no matter where you are on the spectrum, you're aiming for the same place as all of us, which is an increased capacity to access the EM of Self, whether in a group or on your own. And, many people find there is a balance to strike between connecting with Self while alone and connecting as part of a community or group.

Finding this balance is not a "once and done" kind of thing. In fact, it's always evolving for you, depending on your stage of development and the realities around you.

In my own life, I've found that there have been stretches of time when I've deeply valued my own personal yoga practice and other times when I've gotten so much more when practicing amongst others.

And, you may also find yourself very close to the midpoint at times, or vacillating between the two ends of the spectrum, like a pendulum over the mid-point between the two. This is to say that you may desire a mixture of time spent alone, accessing Self and time spent with others who share a similar aim. Wherever you are, in discerning where you are, you actually already begin to open the portal wider to the Self.

AVOIDING THE PITFALL

One of the side effects of engaging in Committed Action mode for the Self is that we can get so enamored with the energy of this EM (it is a very intoxicating energy) that we forget that we are in human form and have an ego. And so, we can get lost in magical thinking or fantasyland and lose our grounding, which can be dangerous to our physical, emotional, or mental well-being.

It is for this reason that, especially the first time you engaged in Committed Action mode for Self, that you simultaneously engage, at least at the level of Awareness mode, if not in Committed Action mode, with one of the other EM's.

Let's get practical! The following exercises are focused on strengthening the force of the soul shower while simultaneously building a bigger bucket to store that energy in.

> "We each have a unique learning style. I recommend that, if after a day or two, you are not expanding your level of awareness, you change the exercise that you are engaging with. Please refer to the Resources&References section, under the header for Chapter 5, to learn more about different learning styles."

A Month of Meditation

Using an entire moon cycle as a container for something extraordinary to happen in the realm of Self can produce amazing results, if you commit to it. If you add to that a practice that is designed to neutralize the ever-present mind, you're starting to "cook with gas." And then, giving ourselves a Calendar month (which averages 30 and ½ days, whereas a Lunar month averages 29 and ½ days) leaves some breathing room for the fact that you are indeed human and may miss a day.

You can choose the kind of meditation that most calls to you. Please turn to the Resources section to tap into one or more of them. Broadly, they fall into three categories: Energetic, Mantric, and Awareness focused. Energetic meditation involves action in the body as well as presence in the mind. Mantric involves, you guessed it, repetition as a way to busy the mind long enough to allow something from Self to surface or sink in. And Awareness involves a careful attention to and focus on the de-identifying process, where thoughts become witnessed as projections onto the movie screen of your mind.

It's critical that you begin with a short meditation and gradually build up the amount of time you are able to spend. And, also, that you begin in a way that is maximally comfortable for the body. It's equally important to, as soon as possible, begin testing the limits of the length of time and your capacity to sit, unsupported with your spine aligned in its natural, vertical position.

Spending Time With God's Canvas

We spend an incredible percentage of our time with absolutely no contact with the actual Earth we are on or even a view that is 100% natural. Mostly, when we look out a window, at best, we see things that are human made mixed in amongst the natural. This exercise involves going somewhere, alone, 2 to 4 times a week, where you can be in the presence of only naturally existing things. If you do not have access to this, you are encouraged to even just get outside and feel whatever weather is happening (sun, rain, or wind). If the weather is of a kind that precludes you being outside long enough to connect to the EM of Self, then, and only then, can you default to spending time inside with some kind of artistic or human created experience that gives you access to either creativity (e.g. an art museum) or pure love (e.g. a dog rescue).

I recommend having no more than one friend with you, and only if without having someone else there, you won't do it. And, if you do have a friend come along, do ensure you spend some of the time on your own as well. Do "de-brief" at the end of the experience to acknowledge the value of what you each experienced.

Bucket List

You likely have seen (or heard of) the movie with Morgan Freeman and Jack Nicholson. While you may not be a Hollywood movie star, you get to create a list of 10 experiences you want to have before you die. But that's not all. What you then need to do is take some kind of action on one of them 3 times per week. It doesn't have to be the same one for all three actions. And, an "action" does include sharing your list or one of the items on your list with someone or researching online. What's important here is that you are not only being present to the fact that this life will be finite, which opens a direct portal to the EM of Self, but also taking action to deal with that reality.

Speaking To Yourself From Self Instead of Mind

Now this one is a bit wacky. But, I know some of you are a bit wacky yourselves. If that's you, here's what to do: start the day by recording into an audio recorder (can be on your smartphone, computer, or even online (check the Resources chapter for a recommended site). What you are recording can be one of the following:

- ○ what your dreams were and what you imagine was being communicated through them from your Self
- ○ what the 10-year-old you would be happy with you doing at some point today
- ○ the three things you are most grateful for even if nothing else happens today

When I say start the day, I literally mean, do nothing else before making this recording, including using the bathroom or drinking water. Well, you can stretch and put your slippers on if you like. But that's it! Listen to the tape as many times as you like during the day. But, for sure, at least once.

Do YourSelf

This one is for the "get moving", action-oriented ones among you. You've got options:

○ You can self create a yoga practice from scratch. I recommend you do this only if you've been practicing for a long time, and it's always a good idea to run it by a trained instructor before engaging with it. It would be smart to begin very simply, perhaps only 5 to 10 basic *asanas*. And then, as you begin to feel what's natural, you'll improvise and add to that core until you have multiple options.

○ You can purchase the book "The 12 Stages of Healing" by Donald Epstein and read about and then practice Stage 9, 10, 11 or 12.

○ You can attend (virtually or in-person) a yoga class that includes practice beyond just the physical *asanas*. I recommend a beginner Kundalini class as a good place to start if you want a direct energetic connection to Self. There are many other types of yoga that may also appeal and/or be effective for you, depending on where you are at and what you've experienced up until this point.

Immerse Yourself In Spirit

Let's get you swimming in the vast, limitless visual and auditory realms. Choose one of the two following options:

○ Watch one video each day, for 30 days, that opens your heart. You may find that you need to create a folder in your Internet browser to capture new ones as you become aware of them. This can be something excellent to do as you transition from work to relaxation (as in, when you return from the office, or, if you work at home, when you shift from an intense period of focus to a portion of the day when you allow yourself to be in the flow). This is not simply a heart warming video, but one that actually opens your heart so that you are left speechless and grateful to have witnessed what is being depicted. Yes, a high standard, but they exist. You can join the online community at www.consciousliving. ning.com to both contribute to and access the growing library of such videos.

○ Listen to music that you feel takes you to another place or gives you a different thought pattern. There are so many artists to choose from. It can be powerful to choose a particular time of day that is sacred for you and then create a habit. For example, in the morning, as you prepare and eat your breakfast (or at some other time that feels right to you). Snatum Kaur is one artist that I particularly appreciate for her ability to assist me in connecting with the EM of Self, through both lyrics and voice.

Remember, these exercises are my best suggestions for dealing directly with the energetic magnifiers. You are welcome to leverage exercises or modalities that you are already familiar with, search out new ones, or create your own! For the most up-to-date thinking on all of these exercises and to share your experience or get support, you can head over to www.consciousliving.ning.com and register for access to the online community.

CHAPTER 14

EPILOGUE

As I reflect on my journey these last 13 years, I have some closing words of wisdom, some of which I've said in other ways throughout the book, and some of which are new.

There is one thing you must get absolutely clear for yourself. Accessing the energy you crave and generating satisfaction in life does not mean you are always going to be happy. I say this because it's what I've observed with the thousands of people I've worked with and in my own life as well. But, you can be satisfied with your life, even when you're not particularly happy.

I want to take a moment to really define what I'm talking about when I'm talking about satisfaction because I'm using this word in a particular way and it may not be the classic definition. The way that I'm defining satisfaction is something like when you lay your head down on your pillow at night just before you're going to fall asleep. When you're satisfied with the way you are living, you might have a thought like, "Wow! Maybe today didn't go exactly as I planned. Not everything happened the way that I had thought it would have when I woke up. It wasn't all tulips and rainbows, but everything unfolded the way it needed to for my life at this moment in time."

That's the kind of experience I'm talking about when we're talking about satisfaction. It's really different and distinct from the emotion of happiness or even contentedness. It's this view that you have of yourself, this context that you have for your life that, "Everything that did happen, happened in a way that was perfect for me in this moment." This is what I'm calling satisfied.

For some people it's more like a feeling in your body; for other people it's more conceptual. That's really the experience I want people to have on a more and more regular basis—this experience of satisfaction. When you can have that experience in life, the emotional landscape can be highly variable over the course of your day, week, and month and your thinking can sometimes get cloudy and disempowered; yet you maintain some kind of deep foundation for satisfaction underneath that which helps you weather all of the bumps on the road of life. So I'm really talking about cultivating a satisfaction that is imperturbable. And, it really does require cultivation. The default experience of life is highly random and mostly chaotic.

During the year since this project began, there have been some major upheavals in my life. I separated from my partner of seven years, experienced a stroke, and I said goodbye to the patriarch of my family, my grandfather Michael Ursitti. What these experiences have shown me, once again, is that no matter how much energy and satisfaction we generate, there will be emotions that are not pleasant. **And,** disempowered thinking will very likely be experienced in this lifetime. You will also experience bodily limitations or breakdowns and may even have a "crisis of the Self" at one or more points. In fact, to not have these things occur might actually be antithetical to one of the main purposes of being alive, which is to experience the full range of what a human is capable of experiencing and also live to tell the tale.

In fact, there will be more to learn for as long as you are embodied. All the more reason to create and nurture your relationship with each of the Energy Magnifiers, so that you can have access to the energy you want to meet the circumstances of your life and, indeed, even *consciously create* the circumstances from time to time.

As you both deepen your connection to (and expand your expression of the energy of) each of these Energy Magnifiers, you will begin to see that there are times when different ones are more "up" for you. So, you can keep coming back to this book and engage with the one or ones that are up for you at that time.

Now, you might be asking yourself the question "Why do different EM's come up at different times?" While there may be an answer to that question, it won't be as important 1to have that answer if all 4 EM's are fully charged for you. If you find yourself stuck with this question, or any question for that matter, for too long, I suggest you take an action or shift something up in your life

When you've got all 4 EM's humming along, or even if you don't, there's something else you'll likely notice. There will be areas of your life that, if they are not fully energized, will drag down the level of satisfaction in other areas of your life. As you learn about your particular "hierarchy of satisfaction," you'll experience the reverse, or "overflow," effect of energy springing from one of the areas of life and raining down on other areas. For example, when I get clear about what's next for me in the realm of career, or simply take committed action in that area, I experience a surge of energy and satisfaction that overflows to the areas of relationship, finance, and even health.

I also invite you to look for actions to take or ways to set things up in your life so that you are engaging with more than one EM at a time. There may be some activities you engage with that give you access to more than one EM. For me, it's yoga. When I practice yoga, I am, at different times, focused on the benefits in my body, the opening to emotion that sometimes occurs, the mental clarity and sometimes even my Self (that animates all the rest). So, for me, yoga is a regular practice I have kept for 13 years and counting.

One last thing. And I don't finish with this thought lightly. It's not very likely at all that you'll be able to generate and maintain a lasting connection to the EMs on your own. So, having partners on the path, identifying powerful mentors, and developing a strong relationship with your word (keeping promises you make to yourself, as well as to others) will all be vitally important. Equally as important is to not get down on yourself when you slip up. You are human. You are not perfect. When you get that you are not perfect, you are once again perfect. Don't ask me. I didn't make up the rules. ☺

RESOURCES & REFERENCES

In our increasingly digital and changeable world, it's possible that some of these will not be in existence in the same way they were when this book was initially published. If that's the case, I invite you to email us at info@awellworld.com and we'll point you in the right direction.

> **RESOURCES = ○**
> **REFERENCES = ●**

Chapter 3

○ For More On SRI : http://www.wiseworldseminars.com/wws/SomatoRespiratoryIntegration/WhatisSRI/index.cfm

Chapter 5

● Dr. Dan Siegel, "The Healthy Mind Platter", http://www.drdansiegel.com/resources/healthy_mind_platter/

● Prashnig, Barbara, "The Power of Diversity", Network Educational Press Ltd

○ The "Hot Towel Scrub" document from IIN® is available at www.consciousliving.ning.com. To access this content, you will need to register as a member and then look for the Forum that is related to Body.

● For More Information on Ishnaan (Cold Showering): Yogi Bhajan, PhD, "The Aquarian Teacher", Kundalini Research Institute, p. 248-249

● Immune/Lymphatic System Support: Scrivens, Dave, "Rebounding: Good for the Lymph System", Well Being Journal, Vol. 17, No. 3.

○ Main, Emily. "5 Ways To Give Yourself An Awesome Massage", Prevention, October, 2012, <http://www.prevention.com/health/health-concerns/self-massage-5-ways-give-yourself-massage>

○ More on NLP (& Other) Learning Styles: https://www.td.org/
Publications/Books/ASTD-Learning-System/~/media/0DBC1BEC809A
403E9396FA0A25F0EB9B.ashx

Chapter 6

Movie Scenes for Different Emotions:

Joy

○ Patch Adams, "Pool of Noodles" Scene -
https://www.youtube.com/watch?v=t5RN8cYKCJ4

○ Footloose, "Final Dance" Scene -
https://www.youtube.com/watch?v=JyD8BxoB2To

Fear

○ Alien, "Chestburster" Scene -
https://www.youtube.com/watch?v=tRX2ntm2rXQ

○ Jurassic Park, "Kitchen" Scene -
https://www.youtube.com/watch?v=hzIVwpCcgkM

Sadness

○ Bambi, "Mother Dies" Scene –
https://www.youtube.com/watch?v=JTZPMJj-X9M
○ Lion King, "The Death of Mufasa" Scene –
https://www.youtube.com/watch?v=LGtJn-L5xEs

Anger

○ The Color Purple, "Hell No" Scene -
https://www.youtube.com/watch?v=Iy2GKyD2IoQ
○ Cinderella, "Stepsisters Tear the Dress" Scene –
https://www.youtube.com/watch?v=R6gSiaAXz1c

○ The SRI Exercise referenced is available at
www.consciousliving.ning.com. To access this content, you will
need to register as a member and then look for the Forum that is
related to Emotions. If you have any trouble finding the file, you
will able to post a question for support in finding it.

Chapter 8

● Lazar, Sarah W. et. al, "Meditation experience is associated with increased cortical thickness" *Neuroreport* 16.17 (2005): 1893-1897. Print. Accessed at <http://www.ncbi.nlm.nih.gov/pmc/articles/PMC1361002/>

● Davidson, R. J., Kabat-Zinn, J., Schumacher, J., Rosenkranz, M. A., Muller, D., Santorelli, S. F., Urbanowski, F., Harrington, A., Bonus, K., & Sheridan, J. F. (2003).Alterations in brain and immune function produced by mindfulness meditation. Psychosomatic Medicine, 65, 564-570, <http://www.investigatinghealthyminds.org/ScientificPublications/2003/DavidsonAlterationsPsychosomaticMedicine.pdf>

● Miller, John J., M.D., Fletcher, Ken, Ph.D., Kabat-Zinn, Jon, Ph.D. (1995). Three year follow-up and clinical implications of a mindfulness meditation-based stress reduction intervention in the treatment of anxiety disorders. General Hospital Psychiatry, Volume 17, Issue 3, 192-200. <http://www.sciencedirect.com/science/article/pii/016383439500025M>

● Koole, Sander L. (2009). Pulling yourself together: Meditation promotes congruence between implicit and explicit self-esteem. Journal of Experimental Social Psychology, 45, Issue 6, 1220-1226. <http://www.sciencedirect.com/science/article/pii/S0022103109001310>

● Lippelt DP, Hommel B and Colzato LS (2014) Focused attention, open monitoring and loving kindness meditation: effects on attention, conflict monitoring, and creativity – A review. Front. Psychol. 5:1083. doi: 10.3389/fpsyg.2014.01083

○ Jumping Off Points Into The World of Breath Exercises:

Pranayama - https://www.youtube.com/watch?v=Xcladu6brgA

Weil - http://www.drweil.com/drw/u/ART00521/three-breathing-exercises.html

Deepak Chopra - https://www.youtube.com/watch?v=y7KeEBevupk

Dalai Lama - https://www.youtube.com/watch?v=BSndVZIAZYc

○ For More on Reiki: http://www.reiki.org/faq/whatisreiki.html
Gyan Mudra: http://www.yogawiz.com/yoga-mudra/gyan-mudra.
html

○ Om Namah Shivaya: http://www.ancientsacredknowledge.com/
hindu/om-namah-shivaya/

Chapter 9

○ More About Marilena Minucci: http://quantumcoachingmethod.
com/

● Doran, G. T. (1981). "There's a S.M.A.R.T. way to write
management's goals and objectives". Management Review(AMA
FORUM) 70 (11): 35–36.

○ More About Peter Drucker: http://www.druckerinstitute.com/
peter-druckers-life-and-legacy/

○ Landmark Education: http://www.landmarkworldwide.com/

Chapter 10

○ Link to SRI Workbook: http://www.wiseworldseminars.com/
utility/showProduct/index.cfm?objectID=302

○ Online Audio Recording: Vocaroo.com

○ A Place To Start With Cleansing: http://www.cleanprogram.com/

○ A Starter Guide for Food Toxicity: http://www.ewg.org/foodnews/
list.php

○ More on Pranayama: http://www.yogapoint.com/info/pranayama.
htm

○ More on Tai Chi Breathing: http://www.beginnerstaichi.com/tai-
chi-breathing.html

○ Qigong Breathing Demonstration: https://www.youtube.com/
watch?v=DZRiHDrhJZY

○ Quality Online Yoga: https://www.yogaglo.com/

○ For Inspiration Around (and Virtual Led Classes) Strength
Training or Cardiovascular Fitness: www.fitnessblender.com

Chapter 11

○ Plutchick's Full List of Emotions:

Acceptance, Trust, Admiration (In Order, from Less to More Intense)

Submission

Apprehension, Fear, Terror (In Order, from Less to More Intense)

Awe

Distraction, Surprise, Amazement (In Order, from Less to More Intense)

Disapproval

Pensiveness, Sadness, Grief (In Order, from Less to More Intense)

Remorse

Boredom, Disgust, Loathing (In Order, from Less to More Intense)

Contempt

Annoyance, Anger, Rage (In Order, from Less to More Intense)

Aggressiveness

Interest, Anticipation, Vigilance (In Order, from Less to More Intense)

Optimism

Serenity, Joy, Ecstasy (In Order, from Less to More Intense)

Love

Chapter 12

○ A list of wisdom leaders follows. Of course, no list of this kind is complete, as there are so very many wise people who have lived or are living. What distinguishes who I saw as eligible for the list and who was not is that those on this list lived (or are living) their awareness and did not solely understand something profound on an intellectual level (in alphabetical order):

  ○ Buddha
  ○ Byron Katie
  ○ Christ
  ○ Deepak Chopra
  ○ Gandhi

○ Louise Hay
○ Marianne Williamson
○ Marshall Rosenberg
○ Maya Angelou
○ Mother Theresa
○ Nelson Mandela
○ Ram Das
○ Rumi
○ Thích Nhâ´t Hạnh

○ More On Non-Verbal Communication: http://en.wikipedia.org/wiki/Nonverbal_communication

○ More About Raven Dana: http://stresswizardcoaching.com/

○ Chapman, Gary D., The 5 Love Languages: The Secret To Love That Lasts, 2010

Chapter 13

○ Options for Different Kinds of Meditation Practice:

Energetic – http://www.3ho.org/3ho-lifestyle/healthy-happy-holy-lifestyle/healthy/ra-ma-da-sa-sa-say-so-hung-ultimate-healing-tool

Mantric – http://www.wildmind.org/mantras

Awareness – This is about cultivating a single point of focus. You can focus on a specific object, sound (this can be the sound of your breath) or on counting to a certain number repeatedly. For more on single point of focus meditation:
http://www.lamayeshe.com/?sect=article&id=407
and
http://www.the-guided-meditation-site.com/candle-meditation.html

○ For More About Snatum Kaur: http://www.snatamkaur.com/

General

○ List of Organizations Providing Foundational Wisdom For Your Empowered Living:

Cherdi Kala - http://www.cherdikala.eu/
IIN - http://www.integrativenutrition.com/
Landmark - http://www.landmarkworldwide.com/)
WiseWorld - http://www.wiseworldseminars.com/

ACKNOWLEDGEMENTS:

Teachers/Mentors

Elena Brower (http://elenabrower.com/)

Raven Dana (http://stresswizardcoaching.com/)

Donald Epstein & Wise World Seminars
(http://www.wiseworldseminars.com/)

Michael Kupferburg (http://www.iloveyoga.com/)

Joshua Rosenthal & The Institute for Integrative Nutrition®
(http://www.integrativenutrition.com/)

Michael Angelo Ursitti, Sr. (heaven)

Multiple Landmark Worldwide Bodies: Advanced Course Leader,
Communication Curriculum Leader, Course Supervisor, Forum
Leader, SELP Leader, Wisdom Course Leader
(http://www.landmarkworldwide.com/)

Supporters

There were certain people who were there for me, during the
sometimes mind-blowing experience of writing this book.
Sometimes for laughs, sometimes for some cheerleading, sometimes
for a bit of tough love. They are, in alphabetical order:

Suzanne Boothby

Seth Braun

Cedric Fokbor

Hugo Larinier

Kyle Shull

IndieGoGo

There were 153 contributions to this book before a word was written, as part of a crowd-sourcing/funding that occurred in late 2013. What follows are the names of people (in order of receipt of contribution) who not only contributed financially, but believed something about what this project represents and/or believed in the value I had to offer:

Ana M Chapaprieta	Kathy Geist	Michael Forman
DanaWyn Sherman	Ellen Allard	Jolene Anello
Amy Simpkins	Ceci Miller	Emma Kareliussen
Eric Eckstein	Chris Bowser	Caroline Webb
Alex Loucopoulos	Andrew Smith	Matthew Howe
Darin Mazepa	Shawn Thompson	Aliza Zaleon
Shannon Werner	Beth Lakretz	Ophira Edut
Seth Braun	David Malcolm Hill	Kate Marcin
Nicolas Ivanhoe Hernandez	Ian Bryce	Tim John
Lori Hamilton	Christopher Amundson	Joanne Schneider
Mia Morgan	Leah Fox	Terrie Lewine
Benjamin Rhatigan	Douglas Dunn	David Nathan
Kim Bradley	Kelli McNamara	Shannon O'Kelly
Tara Mullaney	Ikamara Larasi	Dr. Krishan Ramyead
Yann Leclercq	Blayne Ross	Annick Bonnard
Caitlin & Steve Hartman	Regine Zamor	Charles Scopoletti
Alexandre Emery	Cliff Inkles	Jeannie Advincula
Justin Oliver	Julie Viellieu Thompson	Lucy West
Remy Dresschers	Grace Saccardo	Stacey DePolo
Leora Edut	Karl Henrik Jaeger	Markos Dimitrakopoulos
Ellen Weissbuch	Lee Ang	Elias Ursitti
Angie Dairou	Elena Brower	Rachel P Green
Jared Gruhl	Patrick Rodey	Hugo Larinier
Gordon Shull	Jessica Gilhooley	Dana and Jean-Michel
Kristin Shull	Preeta Sinha	Fonteneau
Celine Renaud	Jacob Voorhees	Kimberly Cox
Lindsay Sklar	Lawrence Damian Pelliccione	Jennifer Ruggiero
Kyle Shull	Nicole Anello	Ken Crease
Alison Gunusen	Michael McCracken	Cédric Fokbor
Geraldine Anello	Helen Vidotto	Sara Wolff
Johnna Macinic	Seth Braun	Emily Shaw
Rachael Talbot	Michelle Rex	Gina Santangelo
Debby Solomon	Virginie Maignal	Liviu Rusu
Rebecca Jackson		
Christopher DeBernardo		
Daniela Pintabona		**Continues on following page**

Sarah Simpson
Colleen Price
Pauline Chow
Donna Tipton
Natalie Buehlmann
Lisa O'Brien
Amy Moberger
Kim Benjamin
Elizabeth Breedlove
Manel Grau
Alicia Fierce
Julie Ann Davis
Karim Herdsman
Lori Hamilton
Shoghik Khachatryan
Dan Lynch
Emily Leather
Justin Oliver
Heather Gifford
Katie Burnett
Graham Staples
Matthew Krug
Anna Wrobel
Marcie Hartman
George Ortiz
Joseph Battisti
Malin Johannesson
Thomas Galati
Derrick Dike
Monica Thompson

Suzanna Russo
Sharon Ramsey & Bruce Curtis
Kristie Valentine
James Stedman & Laurena
Brittain
Nicole Villamora
Annie Stein
Justin & Valerie Ware
Margie Takeda
Barbara Thurlow
David R Breitbach
Meylin Maldonado
Lauren Giacopino
Mala Grewal
Kim Bradshaw
Matt Lyon
Jennifer Beck
+5 Others Who Prefer Not To
Be Publicly Acknowledged

"The following pages are designed for you to be able to rip it out of the book. All physical things are temporary. So, I invite you to be willing to rip this page out, in service of your growth and evolution, and so that it's easier to have with you, on your person, in your actual lived life. Another option, if this is not something you're willing to do, is to write on this page (in pencil if you like) and then take a picture with your mobile device, if you normally have that with you.

Area of Life Satisfaction Ratings

Health/Well-Being:_____

Finances: _____

Intimate Relationship:_____

Career/Job:_____

Family Relationships:_____

Social Life/Friends: _____

Other (_____): _____

Life Overall: _____

Area of Life To Focus On: _____

Current Satisfaction Rating Specific To Area of Life (1-10):_____

Energy Magnifier Ratings (Generally, in Life)

Body: _____

Emotions: _____

Mind:_____

Self:_____

My Strongest EM Is: _____ My Weakest EM Is: _____

Energy Magnifier Ratings (Specific to The Area of Life I'm Focused on Increasing Satisfaction In)

Body:_____

Emotions:_____

Mind: _____

Self: _____

My Strongest EM Is: _____ My Weakest EM Is:_____

Exercise I'm Going To Begin Experimenting With: _____

Actions To Take (When Energy Becomes Available): _____

Area of Life Satisfaction Ratings

Health/Well-Being:_____

Finances: _____

Intimate Relationship:_____

Career/Job:_____

Family Relationships:_____

Social Life/Friends: _____

Other (_____): _____

Life Overall: _____

Area of Life To Focus On:_____

Current Satisfaction Rating Specific To Area of Life (1-10):_____

Energy Magnifier Ratings (Generally, in Life)

Body: _____

Emotions: _____

Mind:_____

Self:_____

My Strongest EM Is: _____ My Weakest EM Is: _____

Energy Magnifier Ratings (Specific to The Area of Life I'm Focused on Increasing Satisfaction In)

Body:_____

Emotions:_____

Mind: _____

Self: _____

My Strongest EM Is: _____ My Weakest EM Is:_____

Exercise I'm Going To Begin Experimenting With: _____

Actions To Take (When Energy Becomes Available): _____

Area of Life Satisfaction Ratings

Health/Well-Being:_____

Finances: _____

Intimate Relationship:_____

Career/Job:_____

Family Relationships:_____

Social Life/Friends: _____

Other (_____): _____

Life Overall: _____

Area of Life To Focus On: _____

Current Satisfaction Rating Specific To Area of Life (1-10):_____

Energy Magnifier Ratings (Generally, in Life)

Body: _____

Emotions: _____

Mind:_____

Self:_____

My Strongest EM Is: _____ My Weakest EM Is: _____

Energy Magnifier Ratings (Specific to The Area of Life I'm Focused on Increasing Satisfaction In)

Body:_____

Emotions:_____

Mind: _____

Self: _____

My Strongest EM Is: _____ My Weakest EM Is:_____

Exercise I'm Going To Begin Experimenting With: _____

Actions To Take (When Energy Becomes Available): _____

Area of Life Satisfaction Ratings

Health/Well-Being:_____

Finances: _____

Intimate Relationship:_____

Career/Job:_____

Family Relationships:_____

Social Life/Friends: _____

Other (_____): _____

Life Overall: _____

Area of Life To Focus On: _____

Current Satisfaction Rating Specific To Area of Life (1-10):_____

Energy Magnifier Ratings (Generally, in Life)

Body: _____

Emotions: _____

Mind:_____

Self:_____

My Strongest EM Is: _____ My Weakest EM Is: _____

Energy Magnifier Ratings (Specific to The Area of Life I'm Focused on Increasing Satisfaction In)

Body:_____

Emotions:_____

Mind: _____

Self: _____

My Strongest EM Is: _____ My Weakest EM Is:_____

Exercise I'm Going To Begin Experimenting With: _____

Actions To Take (When Energy Becomes Available): _____

Area of Life Satisfaction Ratings

Health/Well-Being:_____

Finances: _____

Intimate Relationship:_____

Career/Job:_____

Family Relationships:_____

Social Life/Friends:_____

Other (_____): _____

Life Overall:_____

Area of Life To Focus On:_____

Current Satisfaction Rating Specific To Area of Life (1-10):_____

Energy Magnifier Ratings (Generally, in Life)

Body: _____

Emotions: _____

Mind:_____

Self:_____

My Strongest EM Is: _____ My Weakest EM Is: _____

Energy Magnifier Ratings (Specific to The Area of Life I'm Focused on Increasing Satisfaction In)

Body:_____

Emotions:_____

Mind: _____

Self: _____

My Strongest EM Is: _____ My Weakest EM Is:_____

Exercise I'm Going To Begin Experimenting With: _____

Actions To Take (When Energy Becomes Available): _____

Area of Life Satisfaction Ratings

Health/Well-Being:_____

Finances: _____

Intimate Relationship:_____

Career/Job:_____

Family Relationships:_____

Social Life/Friends: _____

Other (_____): _____

Life Overall: _____

Area of Life To Focus On: _____

Current Satisfaction Rating Specific To Area of Life (1-10):_____

Energy Magnifier Ratings (Generally, in Life)

Body: _____

Emotions: _____

Mind:_____

Self:_____

My Strongest EM Is: _____ My Weakest EM Is: _____

Energy Magnifier Ratings (Specific to The Area of Life I'm Focused on Increasing Satisfaction In)

Body:_____

Emotions:_____

Mind: _____

Self: _____

My Strongest EM Is: _____ My Weakest EM Is:_____

Exercise I'm Going To Begin Experimenting With: _____

Actions To Take (When Energy Becomes Available):_____

Area of Life Satisfaction Ratings

Health/Well-Being:_____

Finances: _____

Intimate Relationship:_____

Career/Job:_____

Family Relationships:_____

Social Life/Friends: _____

Other (_____): _____

Life Overall: _____

Area of Life To Focus On: _____

Current Satisfaction Rating Specific To Area of Life (1-10):_____

Energy Magnifier Ratings (Generally, in Life)

Body: _____

Emotions: _____

Mind:_____

Self:_____

My Strongest EM Is: _____ My Weakest EM Is: _____

Energy Magnifier Ratings (Specific to The Area of Life I'm Focused on Increasing Satisfaction In)

Body:_____

Emotions:_____

Mind: _____

Self: _____

My Strongest EM Is: _____ My Weakest EM Is:_____

Exercise I'm Going To Begin Experimenting With: _____

Actions To Take (When Energy Becomes Available): _____

Area of Life Satisfaction Ratings

Health/Well-Being:_____

Finances: _____

Intimate Relationship:_____

Career/Job:_____

Family Relationships:_____

Social Life/Friends: _____

Other (_____): _____

Life Overall: _____

Area of Life To Focus On: _____

Current Satisfaction Rating Specific To Area of Life (1-10):_____

Energy Magnifier Ratings (Generally, in Life)

Body: _____

Emotions: _____

Mind:_____

Self:_____

My Strongest EM Is: _____ My Weakest EM Is: _____

Energy Magnifier Ratings (Specific to The Area of Life I'm Focused on Increasing Satisfaction In)

Body:_____

Emotions:_____

Mind: _____

Self: _____

My Strongest EM Is: _____ My Weakest EM Is:_____

Exercise I'm Going To Begin Experimenting With: _____

Actions To Take (When Energy Becomes Available): _____

Area of Life Satisfaction Ratings

Health/Well-Being:_____

Finances: _____

Intimate Relationship:_____

Career/Job:_____

Family Relationships:_____

Social Life/Friends:_____

Other (_____): _____

Life Overall: _____

Area of Life To Focus On: _____

Current Satisfaction Rating Specific To Area of Life (1-10):_____

Energy Magnifier Ratings (Generally, in Life)

Body: _____

Emotions: _____

Mind:_____

Self:_____

My Strongest EM Is: _____ My Weakest EM Is: _____

Energy Magnifier Ratings (Specific to The Area of Life I'm Focused on Increasing Satisfaction In)

Body:_____

Emotions:_____

Mind: _____

Self: _____

My Strongest EM Is: _____ My Weakest EM Is:_____

Exercise I'm Going To Begin Experimenting With: _____

Actions To Take (When Energy Becomes Available): _____

Area of Life Satisfaction Ratings

Health/Well-Being:_____

Finances: _____

Intimate Relationship:_____

Career/Job:_____

Family Relationships:_____

Social Life/Friends: _____

Other (_____): _____

Life Overall: _____

Area of Life To Focus On: _____

Current Satisfaction Rating Specific To Area of Life (1-10):_____

Energy Magnifier Ratings (Generally, in Life)

Body: _____

Emotions: _____

Mind:_____

Self:_____

My Strongest EM Is: _____ My Weakest EM Is: _____

Energy Magnifier Ratings (Specific to The Area of Life I'm Focused on Increasing Satisfaction In)

Body:_____

Emotions:_____

Mind: _____

Self: _____

My Strongest EM Is: _____ My Weakest EM Is:_____

Exercise I'm Going To Begin Experimenting With: _____

Actions To Take (When Energy Becomes Available): _____

9905195R00120

Printed in Great Britain
by Amazon.co.uk, Ltd.,
Marston Gate.